THE QUESTION
THAT NEVER
GOES AWAY

WHY

THE QUESTION
THAT NEVER
GOES AWAY
WHY

PHILIP
YANCEY

ZONDERVAN
BOOKS

ZONDERVAN BOOKS

The Question That Never Goes Away
Copyright © 2013 by Philip Yancey and SCCT

Requests for information should be addressed to:
Zondervan, 3900 *Sparks Dr. SE, Grand Rapids, Michigan 49546*

Zondervan titles may be purchased in bulk for educational, business, fundraising, or sales promotional use. For information, please email SpecialMarkets@Zondervan.com.

ISBN 978-0-310-36767-3 (softcover)
ISBN 978-0-310-36580-8 (audio)
ISBN 978-0-310-33983-0 (ebook)

My heart did heave, and there came forth, O God!
By that I knew that thou wast in the grief. . . .

George Herbert, "Affliction (III)"

Contents

PART 1

Where Is God? / 1

The Question Returns

Christmas, Subdued

PART 2

"I Want to Know Why!" / 13

First the Shaking, Then the Wave

The Face of Tragedy

Why?

Our Only Hope

A Shift in Emphasis

"Look for the Helpers"

Do No Harm

PART 3

When God Overslept / 49

"Why Such Brutality?"

A World Blind and Toothless

Cries for Help

Into the Neighborhood

A Shaft of Hope

Pain Redeemed

Room to Grow

PART 4

Healing Evil / 83

Town of Sorrow

Inside the Firehouse

Faith Challenged and Affirmed

Life Cut Short

Two Universals

Tough Questions

Death Be Not Proud

PART 5

Three Extreme Tests / 115

Acknowledgments / 125

Sources / 127

About the Author / 137

Also by Philip Yancey / 139

PART 1

Where Is God?

My father contracted polio just before my first birthday. Paralyzed from the neck down, he lay immobile in a noisy iron lung machine that helped him breathe. My mother would bring my three-year-old brother and me to the hospital and hold us up to the window of the isolation ward so that by looking in a mirror her husband could catch a glimpse of the sons he could not hold or even touch.

My father had been preparing to go to Africa as a missionary, and when he fell ill several thousand people in a prayer chain resolved to pray for his healing. They could not believe that God would "take" someone so young and vibrant with such a bright ministry future ahead of him. In fact, those closest to him became so convinced he would be healed that they decided, with his consent, to take a step of faith and remove him from the iron lung. Within two weeks, he died. I grew up fatherless, under that cloud of unanswered prayer.

Later, as a young journalist about the same age as my father when he died, I began writing "Drama in Real Life" articles for *Reader's Digest* magazine, profiling people who had survived tragedy. Again and again I heard from my interview subjects that "Christians made it worse" by offering contradictory and confusing counsel.

> God is punishing you.

> No, it's Satan!

> Neither: God has afflicted you out of love, not punishment, for you've been specially selected to demonstrate faith.

> No, God wants you healed!

I had no idea how to respond to these people, and in truth I needed answers for myself too. When I face a bedeviling question, I tend to write about it because the writing process affords me the opportunity to go to experts and libraries and the Bible in search of answers. As a result I wrote my first real book at the age of twenty-seven: *Where Is God When It Hurts?*

Although I have written on many other topics, this question that clouded my childhood and dominated my early writing career has never gone away. I still get a steady stream of responses from people devastated by pain and suffering. Recently I pulled out all the letters I've received from others who struggle with the same question — more than a thousand letters in all. Reading through them again reminded me that pain plays as a kind of background static to many lives. Some people live with illness, chronic physical pain, or the lonely curse of clinical depression. Others feel constant heartache out of concern for loved ones: a spouse battling addictions, children on a path to self-destruction, an Alzheimer's-afflicted parent. In some parts of the world ordinary citizens face daily, profound suffering from poverty and injustice.

In one of the letters I received, a sixteen-year-old girl who had been studying Criminal Forensic Profiling articulated one of the most urgent questions:

> I've been studying murders. I've learned about the victims, their families, and the inconceivable torture that they endured. I'm not talking about martyrs or missionaries who have willingly put their lives on the line for their faith, but rather unsuspecting victims of demented crimes. I believe in a heavenly father who loves his children and wishes good for us all and while I do not believe God caused these things to happen to these people, my struggle in my faith is why he could have helped but did not intervene. So my question is this … If God did not protect those people and innocent children who were tortured (while some even cried out to God to save them) how do I have faith that God will protect me? I want to believe, but I feel like the man in the Bible who said to Jesus, "I believe … but help me with my unbelief."

The Question Returns

I have had some personal experience with pain—broken bones, minor surgeries, a life-threatening auto accident—though I've learned far more by listening to others' stories. When my wife worked as a hospice chaplain, often over dinner she would recount conversations with families who were coming to terms with death. We ate food spiced with tears. And as a journalist I heard heartbreaking stories from many others: parents grieving over their gay son's suicide, a pastor enduring the steady onslaught of the disease ALS, Chinese Christians reliving the brutality of the Cultural Revolution.

Because I keep revisiting the theme of suffering, I am sometimes asked to speak on the question of my first book: "Where is God when it hurts?" I will never forget the day I toured the makeshift memorials that had sprung up like wildflowers on the campus of Virginia Tech and then stood before a thousand students, oh so young, their faces raw with grief over the loss of thirty-three classmates and faculty. Or an eerily similar scene the following year when I planned to speak on an unrelated topic in Mumbai, India, until the terrorist attack on the Taj Mahal Hotel and other sites forced a change in venue and a change in topic—back to the question that never goes away.

In 2012 I spoke to groups on that question three times, in the most daunting circumstances. One event followed a catastrophic natural disaster; one took place in a city ravaged by war; the third was closest to home and, for me, the most poignant.

In March I stood before congregations in the Tohoku region of Japan on the first anniversary of the tsunami that slammed into land with the velocity of a passenger jet, snapping railroad tracks like chopsticks and scattering ships, buses, houses, and even airplanes across the ravaged landscape. In its wake, with 19,000 dead and whole villages swept out to sea, a busy secular nation that normally has no time for theological questions thought of little else.

In October I spoke on the question in Sarajevo, a city that had no heat, fuel, or electricity and little food or water for four years while sustaining the longest siege in modern warfare. Eleven thousand residents died from the daily barrage of sniper fire and from the shells and mortars that fell from the sky like hail. One survivor told me, "The worst thing is, you get used to evil. If we knew in advance how long it would last, we would probably have killed ourselves. Over time, you stop caring. You just try to keep living."

As 2012 drew to a close I accepted perhaps the hardest assignment of all, not in terms of quantity of suffering—can it ever be quantified?—but in the sheer intensity of horror and intimate grief. The weekend after Christmas I addressed the community of Newtown, Connecticut, a town reeling from the senseless slaughter of twenty first-graders and six of their teachers and staff.

A first responder captured the mood. "All of us are volunteers," he said. "I've seen some awful things, but we don't train for something like this—nobody does. And my wife is a teacher at Sandy Hook Elementary School. She knew all twenty children by name, as well as the staff. She was three steps behind the principal, Dawn Hochpsrung, when Dawn yelled, 'Go back, it's a shooter!' After hiding out during the shootings she had to walk past the bodies ..."

He paused a moment to control his voice, then continued. "Everyone experiences grief at some point—in the worst case, the terrible grief of losing a child. I see its impact in my role as first responder, especially after suicides. You live with the grief as if in a bubble, and only gradually reenter the world. You go to the grocery store. You go back to work.

Eventually that outer world takes over more and more of you and the grief begins to shrink. Here in Newtown, we're a small community. Everywhere we go reminds us of what happened. We go to the store and see memorials to the victims. We walk down the street and see markers on the porches of those who lost a child. We can't get away. It's like a bell jar has been placed over the town, with all the oxygen pumped out. We can't breathe for the grief."

My invitation to Newtown came from a longtime friend from England named Clive Calver. He headed British Youth for Christ back in the 1970s when I edited the YFC magazine *Campus Life*. We went separate ways, he to international relief work and I to pursue a career as a freelance writer. Clive now pastors a thriving church of 3,500 situated just outside Newtown. "It's as if I've been training all my life for this role," he said when he called me the week before Christmas. "At World Relief I headed a disaster response team with 20,000 resource people around the world. Now, though, it's my neighborhood and my church members who are directly affected. They're all asking the one question you wrote about years ago, 'Where is God when it hurts?' Could you possibly come and speak to us?"

Christmas, Subdued

For me, Christmas of 2012 was like no other. My own father's death on December 15 had always dampened the Christmas spirit in my childhood home, and now the shootings on December 14 darkened the holiday for an entire nation. It felt like a kick in the gut. What has gone wrong with us and with our country? No one could fathom a young man from a privileged background forcing his way into a school and methodically killing a score of terrified first-graders.

I watched news reports and studied the minute-by-minute timeline of what transpired at the elementary school that day. I read online profiles of each child who died and in the process got to know them by name as well as by face: Catherine with the shocking red hair, Daniel's gap-toothed smile, Emilie's luminous blue eyes, Jesse's mischievous grin. I read about the children's pets, their hobbies, the practical jokes they played on their siblings, their food allergies and favorite sports figures. Lives cut short after a scant six or seven years had still left a mark.

What I heard in Newtown that weekend—the stories, the questions, the cries of confusion and protest—stirred up memories of other responses to suffering I've encountered over the years. Why do bad things happen? Why does God allow evil to take its awful course? What possible good can come from such events? I haven't stopped wrestling with these questions since my first book, and I had to face these questions again while speaking to the Newtown community.

As I headed to Connecticut, the publisher of *Where Is God When It Hurts?* made it temporarily available as a free download. I posted the link on Facebook, and the publisher issued a press release but did not advertise the offer. We expected a few hundred responses, maybe a thousand. Instead, as we later learned, more than a hundred thousand people downloaded the book in a few days. Clearly, others have the same question. And so it was that I decided to set aside other writing projects and revisit the question I first explored more than three decades ago.

Winter lingered in Colorado's high country as I wrote. Even in April 2013 I could see out my window a scene of startling beauty: evergreen trees coated in fresh-fallen snow tinted gold by the morning sun, set against a Colorado sky the color of a tropical ocean. And then I would summon up the faces of anguish I saw in Japan and Sarajevo and Newtown.

Suddenly a new set of faces joined them. On April 15 two immigrants spoiled a day of joy and triumph in Boston by planting bombs near the finish line of the Boston Marathon. A race that had begun somberly, with twenty-six seconds of silence to honor Newtown's victims, ended in unspeakable tragedy. The nation's fifth largest city went under lockdown as police searched for the terrorists who had killed three and wounded hundreds. Two days later a fertilizer plant blew up in the town of West, Texas, killing ten firefighters and five others—a disaster that got short shrift on the news due to the massive manhunt taking place in Boston. Later that same week an earthquake shook Sichuan Province, China, killing almost two hundred and injuring nearly twelve thousand. Clearly, the questions raised about suffering in 2012 did not go away in 2013.

I could write about the question in any given year, in fact, for we live on a fragile planet, marred by disease, floods and droughts, earthquakes, fires, wars, acts of violence, and terrorism. Whether catastrophic or commonplace, suffering always lurks nearby. Every day I get another report from the Caring Bridge website on some friend on life support in a hospital or one recovering from a stroke or battling cancer. What is God up to in such a world?

I am well aware that no book can "solve" the problem of pain. Yet I feel compelled to pass along what I have learned from the land of suffering. If Christians have good news to share, some message of hope or comfort for a wounded world, it must begin here.

PART 2

"I Want to Know Why!"

fell in love with Japan on my first visit, in 1998. When the plane taxis up to the gate, baggage handlers and cleaners all bow in greeting. At the hotel, bellhops rush to carry your suitcase, then politely decline all tips. You pull into a service station and white-gloved attendants, often women, surround your car to fill it with gasoline and wash your windows and headlights. How do they keep their uniforms so spotless? When you leave, they bow deeply and wave goodbye as if you have done them a great favor by allowing them to serve you. Bus and taxi drivers use their spare minutes between fares to polish the bumpers of their vehicles and wipe down the seats. You hear few car horns, even in a congested city like Tokyo, as drivers patiently take turns at intersections.

I have returned three times since on visits hosted by my Japanese publisher. The market for books on Christian themes is small. Only one percent of Japanese people identify themselves as Christians, and most of the churches struggle along with only twenty or thirty worshipers. Although visitors may seek out a Christian church in order to practice English or listen to Western music, a new member is rare.

Japanese respect Christianity—some of their finest novelists have written openly about their faith—but view it as a Western import. In their modern, high-tech society, religion survives mainly as a Buddhist or Shinto relic, not a vibrant part of life.

Before speaking at a church or community gathering I would always meet for a tea ceremony in the host's office, where we would munch on bean-paste sweets and exchange gifts. There, the staff would review a precise program of what would take place: song, three minutes and forty seconds; announcement, two minutes; speech, twenty-seven minutes; conclusion, twenty seconds. I'm not sure the Japanese language has a word for spontaneity.

As I think about Japan, two words stand out: *orderliness* and *beauty*. Over the centuries the Japanese have developed a highly ritualized society. They bow to one another as a mark of respect, always waiting for the senior person to straighten up first. As a visitor, you learn to accept a business card by holding it with both hands in front of you, studying it carefully to demonstrate your interest. In public you never show the soles of your shoes nor put your hands in your pockets. When entering a house or church, you remove your shoes and put on guest slippers.

The bathroom involves another set of rituals. Before entering, you remove your house slippers and put on toilet slippers, plastic models decorated with cartoons of Mickey Mouse or Hello Kitty. (Several times I heard the amusing story of a foreign dignitary who neglected to change back and walked onto the platform in an academic cap and gown wearing toilet slippers.) The commode itself looks like the cockpit of a jet, with a set of controls to extend a seat cover, heat the seat, wash and dry yourself, and numerous other functions I've never dared to try.

Yet underlying this formality is a deep appreciation for beauty. Tea is served in delicate china cups, never Styrofoam or plastic; fresh flowers grace the table. City people dress in the latest fashion, and in some rural areas the women still wear elaborate kimonos. Some Japanese homemakers spend an hour each morning preparing bento lunch boxes for their schoolchildren, arranging the portions of seafood, rice, meat, and vegetables in colorful patterns to resemble cartoon characters, animals, or famous monuments. Every Japanese house fortunate enough to have a yard finds a place for a tiny garden or goldfish pond. And to this day I find it impossible to throw away Christmas cards from Japan, delicate works of art that feature pop-up flowers or kimono designs.

On my latest visit to that exotic and delightful nation, however, I found the opposite of orderliness and beauty. In one horrifying day a tsunami swept aside what Japanese society values most, replacing it with mud, destruction, and trauma.

First the Shaking, Then the Wave

An advancing hurricane you can prepare for by nailing plywood over windows, securing shutters, or, if necessary, evacuating. Ominous skies and weather alerts usually give at least a few minutes' warning of an oncoming tornado. But a tsunami can roll in on a bright, sunny day, and, in a flash, with no forewarning, the solid earth seems to convulse.

On March 11, 2011, at 2:46 in the afternoon, a 9.0 magnitude earthquake shook the east coast of Japan for three to five minutes. Roads buckled, bridges cracked, bookcases toppled, some buildings collapsed. The earthquake had such force that, incredibly, it jolted Japan's largest island some eight feet closer to North America. All was still for forty-five minutes as residents picked themselves up and surveyed the damage.

Then came the wave.

A wall of water, first taking shape far out in the ocean by the quake's epicenter, accelerated to 500 mph as it sped toward land. The coastal region of Tohoku had subsided two feet during the quake, opening wide the gate for the onrushing wave, so that the tsunami crashed over protective sea walls like a giant stepping over a curb. Videos shot on iPhones by eyewitnesses (some retrieved from corpses) resemble the special-effects scenes from a horror movie: ships, houses, and trucks tossed around like toys; a modern airport suddenly submerged under water; a nuclear reactor tower exploding in a thick black cloud.

A British high school teacher heard emergency sirens, looked out on the ocean, and saw a towering mist. "This must have been the spray from the tsunami, but it looked so awesome and strange," he said. "It was as if there had been a massive fire on the ocean, and above it were vast, rolling white clouds of smoke. In it, I could see thousands of bits, floating. They must have been buildings, ships, cars — but they looked so tiny. It was all so awesome that my brain couldn't compute." He led his forty-two students to safety, but more than a hundred others in the school perished that day while dutifully awaiting instructions from their teachers.

A pastor was checking for earthquake damage in his home when he got a frantic text message from his daughter in Tokyo: "Escape! Escape! Escape!" It seemed odd at the time during the forty-five-minute interlude of calm, but without electricity he had no local radio source and so decided to follow her advice to evacuate. Swept along the wave in his car like a surfer, he landed in the midst of a debris field where he lived inside the car for two days before rescuers found him.

Another pastor fled with his wife to high ground after the earthquake. A sudden snow squall hit just as the tsunami approached, and for a few minutes they could see nothing from their safe perch. They heard the wave roll in, then surge back out to sea carrying human bodies and tons of debris, the backwash as dangerous as the initial wave. Seventeen times it rolled in and washed back out, like water sloshing in a bathtub. Sixteen of the times they heard frantic cries for help, then at last a loud sucking sound as if from a huge drain, then silence. When the snow cloud passed, they looked out over a neighborhood utterly destroyed, not a building left, only the cross from their church sticking up at an unnatural angle like a broken bone. A few scraggly trees stood by the beach, sentinels of what the day before had been a dense forest.

When the giant wave found a sheltered cove tucked among hills, it increased in velocity and force as a huge volume of water poured into the narrow opening. On flat land the wave measured ten to thirty feet high; in hilly coves it rose to the unimaginable height of a twelve-story building. Given their history with tsunamis, the Japanese had well-organized evacuation sites—schools, hospitals, senior citizens' centers—and many residents fled to these for shelter when the warning sirens sounded. No one had anticipated a tsunami so colossal, however, and in a cruel irony, many hundreds died in the very buildings meant to save them.

In one senior citizens' center situated high on a hill, forty-seven seniors died; today a pile of wheelchairs, mattresses, and furniture marks a grim memorial. In the same town scores of people climbed to the roof of a three-story evacuation center, but only a few managed to avoid getting swept away by clinging to railings and a television antenna. In an elementary school seventy-four students died as school officials were sorting out procedures for leading them up a hill just behind the school. Some of the children broke free to scramble upward across snowy ground, only to lose their footing and slip into the wave's deadly maw.

The Face of Tragedy

Exactly one year after the earthquake and tsunami, I spent several days visiting the affected area along with some staff from my Japanese publisher. I had never seen such destruction up close. Even a year later the landscape looked sere, barren, as if from another planet. I asked a few questions of my hosts, but mostly I stared out the window and tried to absorb the immensity of their nation's tragedy. Others in the van said little, and I could not read their faces. I thought of the line from the poet Emily Dickinson: "After great pain a formal feeling comes."

My own feelings were far from formal. After touring

the devastated peninsula once known for its quaint fishing villages, I was scheduled to speak on "Where is God when it hurts?" to somber gatherings in the Tohoku region and also at a national prayer meeting in Tokyo. What could I say to such people, a visitor from another country touching down in the midst of their pain? Most Japanese do not even believe in God. How could I point them to the God of grace and mercy I have learned to love, who seemed very far away from such a scene?

The industrious Japanese had repaired or replaced many roads, raising the roadbeds several feet above the sunken land. Crews had removed most of the lumber and rubble from the million damaged buildings; only the most durable structures remained standing, ghost buildings with broken windows and mud-splattered, crumbling walls. Artificial mountains of debris sullied the landscape, some of them seventy feet high and the dimensions of a city block.

Other parts of Japan had resisted accepting the twenty-three million tons of debris for incineration or burial lest it contain contaminants or radiation from the crippled nuclear power plant. "I wonder how many automobiles were destroyed," I said aloud as we passed yet another mound of crushed vehicles. Immediately a Japanese colleague pulled out his smart phone and googled the answer: 410,000.

Driving into one town we turned a corner, and there sat a huge freighter, two-thirds the length of a football field, beached on the concrete foundations of what used to be a residential area. No one could figure out how to get it back to the ocean half a mile away. Some seventeen ships and a thousand smaller fishing boats had washed ashore in that town, and many remained where the tsunami had incongruously deposited them—in the middle of a rice paddy, atop a hotel, on the roof of a hospital.

CNN and other news sources gauge disasters by statistics, and by any measure the tsunami of 2011 ranks as one of the most costly in human lives and financial loss. On the ground, though, I saw the disaster as a collection of individual personal stories, not statistics. The man who watched helplessly from a tall building as his wife and children floated away in their house. Another family whose house slammed into a bridge, giving all eight family members a chance to leap to safety. Seven employees of a fish-processing plant who jumped into a van and drove toward high ground, only to get stuck in traffic gridlock and have the tsunami churn the van like an object in a washing machine, killing five of them.

I spoke with a man who lived on the coast near Sendai and spent four nights on the roof with his wife. Downstairs all was flooded, and the two resorted to eating dog food in order to stay alive. Several times he tried to leave but found it impossible to wade through the chest-high, frigid water. The first time he stepped into the water he felt a sharp pain in his side: falling debris had broken two of his ribs during the earthquake, an injury he had not even noticed. "Mainly I remember the freezing cold," he said. "We shivered in wet clothes, with no heat and no food, waiting for rescue from the roof."

A few heartwarming stories of survival brought hope the first days after the tsunami. An eighty-year-old grandmother and her teenage grandson survived nine days before being discovered, hypothermic but uninjured. A rescue helicopter spotted a sixty-year-old man floating on the roof of his house ten miles offshore. Of course we only hear the stories from survivors and can barely imagine the details of the nineteen thousand who died. Emergency response crews who had geared up to treat the injured found relatively few; such is the force of a tsunami that most of its victims get swept away.

Even now, enormous problems remain. The government is still debating which towns to rebuild and which to abandon as too vulnerable. A cloud of fear and gloom hangs over the entire area. As one counselor told me, "I've learned that PTSD [post-traumatic stress disorder] is a misnomer. After something like the tsunami, that syndrome is a sign of *health*, not a disorder. Who wouldn't feel trauma and stress?" Authorities worry about the Japanese suicide rate, already among the world's highest.

And then there's Fukushima, site of the nuclear power plant that still dominates the news in Japan. As we neared the area, a portable Geiger counter ticked off the amount of microsieverts per hour we were receiving. Unlike the scenes of destruction, in that region houses, shops, temples, and office buildings stand intact, untouched by the wave but void of human inhabitants. Due to radiation and the danger of further meltdown, officials have declared a "no go" zone where only stray animals and abandoned pets wander the streets. Within Japan former residents of Fukushima have become pariahs. Some hospitals refuse to treat them, and other regions hesitate to hire employees from that area. A mortician became a local hero when he agreed to prepare the bodies of those who had died, an important ritual in

Japan, but a job no one dared accept for fear of contamination. "Don't have children!" Fukushima survivors tell their own children, fearful of genetic defects.

Stoical and understated by nature, most survivors related their stories to me in flat, unemotional tones. One woman was different. She had driven more than an hour at night over temporary roads to a service in a church that, its sanctuary destroyed, now meets in a printing plant. In a cosmetic style peculiar to Japan, she wore thick white facial makeup, like a china doll. Her piercing dark eyes rarely blinked. "I was buried in a pile of garbage and rubble for two days!" she said. "Then I saw a hand reaching down like this," and she suddenly seized my hand in a most un-Japaneselike gesture. "I grabbed the hand that pulled me out. I lost everything— my family, my friends, my town. No one wants to go back. The town no longer exists. Please don't forget us! They forgot me for days; now they forget my town. I want to know why!"

Why?

Oh, how we long for an answer to that everlasting question. Sarajevo and other wars we can blame on human evil that has brought about incalculable suffering. Newtown, Boston, and similar tragedies we can blame on mental illness or radical ideology or bad gun laws or negligent parenting. Tsunamis and other natural disasters, absent anyone else to blame, we classify as "acts of God."

Agnostics have a field day after such cataclysmic events. Voltaire and fellow Enlightenment thinkers abandoned belief in "the best of all possible worlds" after an earthquake in 1755 destroyed Lisbon, Portugal, on All Saints' Day. When another tsunami killed 280,000 in Asia the day after Christmas, 2004, *Slate* magazine ran an article titled "Send a Message to God: He Has Gone Too Far This Time." In it, Heather Mac Donald wrote, "It's time to boycott God":

> God knows that he can sit passively by while human life is wantonly mowed down, and the next day, churches, synagogues, and mosques will be filled with believers thanking him for allowing the survivors to survive. The faithful will ask him to heal the wounded, while ignoring his failure to prevent the disaster in the first place....
>
> Where is God's incentive to behave? He gets credit for the good things and no blame for the bad.

David Bentley Hart, an Eastern Orthodox theologian, had the courage to respond to skeptics in a small book titled *The Doors of the Sea: Where Was God in the Tsunami?* Mass tragedies may provoke outrage from unbelievers, he said, but in fact they teach us nothing new about the world we live in. The scale of suffering doesn't change the underlying issues. Suffering, evil, and death blight our planet, and catastrophes simply concentrate the misery we already know so well.

It does not help to try to quantify suffering, I have learned along the way. That the tsunami of 2004 killed far more people than the tsunami of 2011 or that more students died at Virginia Tech than at Sandy Hook Elementary School does not make one event more tragic than the other.

Likewise, to the person with a migraine headache or chronic fatigue syndrome, it does not help to point to someone with a worse condition, say, AIDS or the Ebola virus. All suffering is suffering. As C. S. Lewis said, there is no such thing as "the sum of the world's suffering," an abstraction of the philosophers. There are simply individual people who hurt. And who wonder why God permits it.

Visiting sites of tragedy, I am struck each time by what the news media do to our perceptions. I went to Virginia Tech aware of the thirty-three who died as a collective group, "the worst mass shooting in U.S. history," as television kept repeating. Yet walking among the individual memorials I encountered Ryan and Emily and Juan and Waleed and Julia—thirty-three individuals, not a group. Personal mementoes recalled their distinct lives: a baseball, a teddy bear, a copy of *The Great Gatsby*, a Starbucks cup. I had the same reaction at Newtown, Connecticut, as I met with bereaved families and heard about children's pets and their quarrels with siblings.

In Japan, the cry of the woman with the china-doll face hit me with more eloquent force than any statistic I had read about the tsunami. We experience suffering alone—it "islands" us—and for the people involved, scale doesn't matter so much. Even a mega-disaster like the tsunami zooms in personally: a child swept away from a kindergarten playground, a family business destroyed in an instant, a teenager terrified by the aftershocks that hit weekly, everyone frightened by the invisible threat of radiation.

Theologian Hart goes on to note a secret irony hidden

in the arguments of the skeptics: "They would never have occurred to consciences that had not in some profound way been shaped by the moral universe of a Christian culture." The most strident voices pounce on a mass tragedy as if it puts a final nail in the coffin of belief: How could a good God possibly allow such a calamity? Though the question is unavoidable, and a profound mystery, it applies only in the context of religious faith. I have yet to hear critics offer a response consistent with their own beliefs: *Why are you shocked and upset? What else should we expect from an impersonal universe of random indifference?*

Actually, the Bible presents more potent objections than those of the skeptics. When speaking at universities I sometimes challenge my audience to find an argument against God—whether in the classical atheists Voltaire, Bertrand Russell, and David Hume, or in contemporary ones such as Richard Dawkins, Sam Harris, and the late Christopher Hitchens—not articulated in biblical books. "You are free to reject God and the way this world runs," I tell students tempted to do just that; "I, for one, respect a God who not only gives us the freedom to reject him, even to crucify his Son, but also includes the words of rejection in our Scriptures."

Let me give a brief sampler:

- Gideon (speaking to an angel): "If the LORD is with us, why has all this happened to us?"

- Job: "Though I cry, 'Violence!' I get no response; though I call for help, there is no justice."

- Psalms: "Awake, Lord! Why do you sleep? Rouse yourself!"

- Ecclesiastes: "Utterly meaningless! Everything is meaningless."
- Isaiah: "Truly you are a God who has been hiding himself."
- Jeremiah: "Why are you like a man taken by surprise, like a warrior powerless to save?"
- Jesus: "My God, my God, why have you forsaken me?"

The writer Anne Lamott applauds this vein of protest.

My belief is that when you're telling the truth, you're close to God. If you say to God, "I am exhausted and depressed beyond words, and I don't like You at all right now, and I recoil from most people who believe in You," that might be the most honest thing you've ever said. If you told me you had said to God, "It is all hopeless, and I don't have a clue if You exist, but I could use a hand," it would almost bring tears to my eyes, tears of pride in you, for the courage it takes to get real—really real. It would make me want to sit next to you at the dinner table.

How does the Bible answer such laments? Usually with silence. Job, that unfortunate man who deserved suffering least yet endured it most, finally got his requested audience with God, who responded with his longest recorded speech. Oddly, though, while giving Job a tour of the natural world in magnificent poetry, God never addressed the *Why?* question. In Frederick Buechner's words, "God doesn't

explain. He explodes. He asks Job who he thinks he is anyway. He says that to try to explain the kind of things Job
wants explained would be like trying to explain Einstein to
a littleneck clam.... God doesn't reveal his grand design.
He reveals himself." Then, in a delicious irony, God pro-
nounces that only through Job's advocacy will he listen to
the friends who had badgered Job with their condemnatory
theology. They had begun well, "sitting shiva" with Job for
seven days of silence; the problems began when they opened
their mouths.

I have often wondered why the Bible gives no systematic
explanation for the problem of suffering. The prophets had
a cause-and-effect view of why Israel suffered, but they delivered their warnings well in advance and always with a promised remedy if the nation changed its ways. Jesus brushed
aside questions of cause, except to refute the Pharisees' and
disciples' airtight theories of suffering-as-punishment. Most
biblical authors, it seems, did not sit around scratching their
heads over the question "Why do bad things happen to good
people?" They viewed this world as enemy territory, a spoiled
planet ruled by the father of lies, the wizard of woe. What
else should we expect from Satan's lair? When the prince
of this world offered a tempting shortcut solution to earth's
problems, Jesus did not scoff at his presumption of authority;
he simply chose against it, in favor of a slower, more costly
yet permanent solution.

Japanese Buddhists who take their faith seriously—and
only a minority do—anticipate a time when the souls of
those who die will lose their identity and merge with the one-
ness of the universe. Secular unbelievers resign themselves

to the extinction of the planet millions of years from now when the sun flames out like a dying match. In contrast, Christians place their hope in a time when death, "the last enemy," will be destroyed, when God will sort out evil from good and death from life, and resurrect both bodies and souls in a final resolution: "I am making everything new."

I attended the funeral of a child in Chicago in which the pastor shocked the mourners by glancing down at the coffin and interrupting his eulogy with the sudden exclamation, "Damn you, death!" Catching himself, he quickly added, "Not God—it's death I'm damning. And God too has promised to damn it."

Our Only Hope

We live on a fallen planet, say the theologians. Anyone who doubts that should visit Japan. I have read reports from the seismologists who expected "the big one" to hit not forty-five miles off the coast of Tohoku but farther south near Tokyo, which would have caused far more damage. As it was, the earthquake hit with such force that it caused the earth to shift on its axis, reducing daylight by a few microseconds, upsetting GPS monitoring stations around the world, and releasing six hundred million times the energy of the atomic bombs that fell on Japan in 1945.

The tectonic forces that proved so destructive in 2011, however, are the same ones that formed the islands of Japan in the first place. The hurricanes and cyclones that wreak such havoc are essential to the weather systems that spread moisture across the globe. Seen through any lens, natural or theological, this world is "in process"—flawed, incomplete, imperfect.

Ever since Adam we humans have been assigned the tasks of stewardship: growing gardens among thorns and this-tles, tending the animals, building civilizations. As a species of sub-creators made in God's image, we are charged with bringing order out of chaos. We have made giant strides: until two centuries ago half of all children died before the age of five and the life span of adults averaged thirty-five years. We have tamed rivers, made the sky our highway, devised ways to stay warm in winter and cool in summer, and knit the world together in an electronic web.

Admittedly, these advances have come with a cost: diminishing resources and increased population, pollution and its effect on the climate, injustices that allow some to live in comfort at the expense of others. History marches on, and all this time God has "sat on his hands" charge the crit-ics. God did not intervene when European powers carved up continents and the New World imported millions of slaves, or when Nazis tried to exterminate the "chosen people" in the most notorious of numerous attempts at genocide. For whatever reason, God has chosen to let history take its course.

Why? We have no more definitive answer than Job got. We have only the stubborn hope—so different from naive optimism—that the story of Jesus, which includes both death and resurrection, gives a bright clue to what God will do for the entire planet. Optimism promises that things will gradually improve; Christian hope promises that creation will be transformed. Until then, God evidently prefers not to intervene in every instance of evil or natural disaster, no matter how grievous. Rather, God has commissioned us as agents of intervention in the midst of a hostile and broken world.

"It is for your good that I am going away," Jesus told the mystified disciples in a final act of delegation, giving us the pattern to follow. "I will not speak with you much longer, for the prince of this world is coming. He has no hold on me, but the world must learn that I love the Father and that I do exactly what my Father has commanded me." Then Jesus went out to face a long night of suffering, which he had prayed fervently against and yet would decline to use his power to prevent.

Creation has been groaning "as in the pains of child-birth," Paul told the Romans, harboring no illusions about the state of our planet. Our only hope is radical interven-tion, that one day "the creation itself will be liberated" in a sort of cosmic rebirth. Until then, no answer to suffering will satisfy, even if we had the capacity to comprehend the answer. Like Job, we can only attend to the small picture, clinging to belief against all contrary evidence while trust-ing God with the big picture. Faith, I've concluded, means believing in advance what will only make sense in reverse.

A Shift in Emphasis

Could there be a hidden advantage to the Bible's evading the Why? question? Knowing the answer shifts attention from the one suffering to the circumstances that caused it and in the process does little to help the person in need. For example, Jesus' disciples asked about a man born blind, "Who sinned, this man or his parents?" Choosing either option would hardly have stirred compassion for the blind man; the disciples likely would have clucked their tongues, relished their moral superiority, and walked away with a feeling that the poor guy got what he deserved. Instead, Jesus contradicted such suffering-as-punishment theories—just as God had dismissed them with a scowl at Job's pious friends—and focused on the man's lack of sight.

As if by instinct, after a major disaster we fixate on the cause. Was it the O-rings that caused the *Challenger* spacecraft to explode? Could the FBI have prevented the 9/11 attacks or the Boston Marathon bombings? Would higher sea walls have helped Tohoku? What mental state triggered Adam Lanza's attack on Sandy Hook? Although that approach has great value in preventing future occurrences, it does little for the immediate victims. I think of the Japanese people I met who had to evacuate their homes near the Fukushima nuclear power plant, now living in temporary housing, treated like pariahs, and fearful of imminent health problems. Yes, scientists and engineers need to investigate exactly what design flaws led to a reactor meltdown, but in the meantime, what about the ones suffering?

Virtually every passage on suffering in the New Testament deflects the emphasis from *cause* to *response*. Although we cannot grasp the master plan of the universe, which allows for so much evil and pain (the *Why?* question), we can nevertheless respond in two important ways. First, we can find meaning in the midst of suffering. Second, we can offer real and practical help to those in need.

In his book *The Problem of Pain* C. S. Lewis wrote, "God whispers to us in our pleasures, speaks in our conscience, but shouts in our pains: it is His megaphone to rouse a deaf world." I hesitate to disagree with Lewis, yet that image makes me uncomfortable. It calls to mind a football coach on the sideline yelling at his players through a bullhorn, and some readers may infer from the metaphor that God dishes out suffering to get our attention. I don't think Lewis intended such an inference, and for that reason I would change the image from megaphone to hearing aid. When suffering strikes, it gives us, the afflicted ones, an opportunity to turn up the volume and attend to crucial messages that we might otherwise ignore.

Certainly, I have experienced the amplification value of pain. Breaking my neck in an auto accident in 2007 caused me to reexamine my marriage, my faith, and how I plan to spend the years I have left. As I lay strapped to a backboard awaiting word on whether a major artery had been punctured—in which case, the doctor told me, I had mere minutes to live—I could only think of three questions worth pondering: Who do I love? What have I done with my life? Am I ready for whatever is next? Of course, I could have been aligning my life with those questions all along, but it took a traumatic event for me to tune in to what matters most.

The German poet Rainer Maria Rilke wrote,

Were it possible, we might look beyond the reach of our knowing.... Then perhaps we would endure our griefs with even greater trust than our joys. For they are the moments when something new has entered into us, something unfamiliar.... Everything within us steps back; a silence ensues, and something new ... stands in the center and is silent.

Akin to what Rilke describes, a shift took place among the young people of Japan after the tsunami. For years parents had wrung their hands over the impact on Japan's coddled youth of "the lost decades" of economic stagnation. Japanese sociologists have a catalog of words to describe the misfit generation: *freeters* who deliberately choose unchallenging, dead-end careers; *hikikomori* who isolate themselves, some of them never venturing out of their bedrooms; *parasites* who mooch off their parents for room and board so they can afford the latest electronic gadgets and fashion statements. To everyone's surprise, these floundering young people awoke as if from sleep after the earthquake and tsunami. They volunteered at shelters and food distribution sites, donated money for relief, and used their social-networking skills to reunite the displaced with their families and spur the government to be more forthcoming about the reactor meltdown. They also led the way in heeding the government's save-electricity campaign to compensate for the loss of Japan's nuclear power plants.

Viktor Frankl, a survivor of four different Nazi concentration camps who went on to found a school of psychotherapy, decided that the search to find meaning in life is our most powerful driving force. And, according to Frankl, our response to unavoidable suffering is one of the chief ways of finding that meaning. "Despair is suffering without meaning," he wrote; and "everything can be taken from a man but one thing: the last of the human freedoms — to choose one's attitude in any given set of circumstances."

The citizens of Japan provide a model of how to respond to a major disaster. The news media rightly celebrated the patience and endurance — the long-suffering — of the Japanese people. Residents voluntarily turned in almost a hundred-million-dollars' worth of cash and valuables found in the rubble, in contrast to the looting that occurs in many places after a disaster. For weeks after the tsunami, thousands of evacuees slept in gymnasiums and crowded halls, standing in line for hours to receive a bottle of water and a bowl of rice. When I visited the earthquake zone a year later, a quarter-million Japanese were still living in temporary housing, twelve-by-forty-foot modular units such as you see on construction sites elsewhere. Their response was a dramatic departure from the grousing and lawlessness that followed Hurricane Katrina in New Orleans.

Sadly, Japan has had much experience in recovering from catastrophe: the Kanto earthquake of 1923 killed 140,000 people; the Kobe earthquake of 1995 killed 6,400 and caused one hundred-billion-dollars' worth of damage. Most remarkably, the nation rose from the ashes after World War II, which left behind three million dead and many cities destroyed as well as the ongoing curse of nuclear fallout.

"Look for the Helpers"

A society shows its true strength by how it treats its most vulnerable members, and we in the West have much to learn from the example of Japan. As the misfit generation of Japan learned, the very process of responding to the needy can give a new meaning to life.

The anthropologist Margaret Mead used to ask her lecture audiences, "What would you say is the earliest sign of civilization?" She would field replies such as "a clay pot" or "tools made of iron" or "the first domesticated plant." Then she would say, "Here is my answer," and hold up a human femur, the largest bone in the leg, pointing to a thickened area where the bone had healed after a fracture.

As Mead observed, "Such signs of healing are never found among the remains of the earliest, fiercest societies. In their skeletons we find clues of violence: a rib pierced by an arrow, a skull crushed by a club. But this healed bone shows that someone must have cared for the injured person—hunted on his behalf, brought him food, served him at personal sacrifice." Contrary to nature's rule of "survival of the fittest," we humans measure civilization by how we respond to the most vulnerable and the suffering.

Children's television personality Fred Rogers said that when he was a little boy and heard about an accident or natural disaster, his mother would tell him, "Look for the helpers, Fred. Whenever something terrible happens there are always people who hurry to help." We in the U.S. saw clear examples in the ten firefighters who rushed to a burning fertilizer plant in Texas only to lose their lives in the resulting explosion. And as spectators scattered after the Boston Marathon bombings, medical personnel ran toward the injured, exposing themselves to damage from the second blast. Some runners who had just completed a twenty-six mile race kept running to nearby hospitals in order to give blood. That night, thousands of Boston residents opened their homes to stranded visitors for dinner and lodging.

Newtown, Connecticut, showed a remarkable community response to a disaster very different from the one in Japan, in this case much smaller in scale and directly caused by humans.

A retired psychologist who lived across the street from Sandy Hook Elementary School looked out his window the morning of December 14 and saw the unusual sight of four girls and two boys sitting on his front lawn in the middle of a school day. When he approached them, one little boy explained, "We can't go back to school. Our teacher is dead—Mrs. Soto. We don't have a teacher." The retiree invited the kids inside and brought them toys and juice while he tried to find out what had happened and phoned the authorities. "Being a psychologist had nothing to do with it," he told a news reporter who commended him. "I responded like a grandfather."

Within days of the shooting, hundreds of volunteers swarmed over a vacant school building in a nearby town to ready it for Sandy Hook students. They moved furniture and desks from the old school and decorated the new one to make it look as familiar as possible. A closely knit community, Newtown seems determined to shed its image from a town of sorrow to a town that prevails despite sorrow.

Speaking with some of the families who lost children at Sandy Hook, I heard of the outpouring of concern and compassion by an entire nation. A friend of mine who had moved from Denver to Newtown six months before the shooting, in order to be near his son's family, lost the grand-daughter whose life he had hoped to share. "The community response has been unbelievable," he said. "The state patrol assigned a trooper to each affected family for weeks after the shootings, to help with security and protection from the media, and that trooper has become part of our family. We have freezers full of donated food, more Christmas presents than you can count, and the offer of counseling as long as we need it. Right now my wife and I are busy answering some of the three thousand cards and letters that came to our home expressing sympathy for our loss."

Not all well-meaning expressions of help accomplish their goal. One counselor in Newtown told me, "A lot of the response outside the community seemed more helpful to the givers than the receivers. We had truckloads of teddy bears and stuffed animals shipped in, more than sixty thousand in all. Does any school need sixty thousand stuffed animals? We gave most of them away to homeless shelters for the kids who stay there. People showed up from all over the country with their juggling acts, free pies, pets, advice booths. Food poured in. There are a lot of Italians in the Northeast, and one family with a full freezer begged, 'Please—no more pasta!'"

On the other hand, some outsiders found meaningful ways to express their solidarity. A renowned potter from California began work on memorial vases commemorating each child who died. A quilter in Maryland volunteered to make twenty memorial quilts incorporating photos and mementoes of the children. Portrait artists got together to commission a portrait of each victim. Such gestures gave lasting proof to Newtown that a nation cares about its loss.

One of the most touching gestures came from other schoolchildren. At the suggestion of a Sandy Hook parent, the president of Connecticut's Parent Teacher Student Association sent an email to Connecticut schools asking them to cut snowflakes out of paper to help decorate the new school where Sandy Hook students would attend. The request went viral. Within two days the first box of snowflakes arrived at his office, and soon brown UPS trucks and semi-trailers from the Postal Service were arriving daily to unload thousands upon thousands of boxes from every state and fifty foreign countries. "I had no idea what I was starting," he told CBS cameramen as he stepped around the boxes that filled every corner of the PTSA office and a nearby warehouse. "Literally an avalanche of snow!" After decorating every school in the district, they still had millions left over.

Many of the snowflakes came with handwritten notes from children. Some included piggy bank collections in plastic Ziploc bags, or football and baseball cards. "I feel like crying," said one child. "It's children, just like us." Sometimes awkwardly, sometimes poignantly, healthy communities respond to victims of trauma. The underlying message is simple: *You are not alone.*

Ideally, that principle should apply always, not only in times of major tragedy. A university researching pain recruited volunteers to test how long they could keep their feet in buckets of freezing water. They observed that when a companion was allowed in the room, the volunteer could endure the cold twice as long as those who suffered alone. "The presence of another caring person doubles the amount of pain a person can endure," the researchers concluded. All too often our pain-denying, death-denying culture does just the opposite: we put suffering people in hospitals and nursing homes, isolating them from normal human contact. Two out of three people die in such institutions, often alone.

Every survey shows that a person who is connected with a caring community heals faster and better. Known "enemies of recovery" such as stress, guilt, anger, anxiety, and loneliness are best defeated by a compassionate community. If you don't have to worry about your medical bills or who will look after your children, or even your pets, when you go in for surgery, you will heal better. In one study of patients with metastatic breast cancer, the women who attended a mutual support group every week for one year felt better and lived almost two years longer than the women who did not attend the group, even though both groups received the same chemotherapy and radiation treatment.

Someone asked a Lutheran bishop, "What is the best advice a pastoral or other counselor might give to a woman in her prime who faces devastating health problems?" His answer: "She should have been an active member of a vital congregation for the previous twenty years."

Do No Harm

The apostle Paul said about a healthy community, "If one part suffers, every part suffers with it; if one part is honored, every part rejoices with it." The Christian community, known worldwide by the symbol of a cross and by our regular partaking of a sacrament "in remembrance of me," should be able to make a unique contribution to those who suffer.

Alas, as I have heard repeatedly, all too often "the church made it worse."

When the Indonesian tsunami killed a quarter-million people on a sunny day in 2004, geologists blamed it on the rupture of an undersea mega-thrust on the sea floor, triggering the giant wave. Some televangelists credited it instead to God's wrath against "pagan" nations in that region that had been persecuting Christians. Along the same line, one Christian leader traced the cause of the 2011 Japanese tsunami to the fact that "Japan is under control of the sun goddess." When terrorists killed three thousand people by crashing airplanes into the World Trade Center, a prominent fundamentalist in Virginia blamed it on "the pagans and the abortionists and the feminists and the gays and the lesbians who are actively trying to make that an alternative lifestyle, the ACLU, People for the American Way ... I point the thing in their face and say, you helped this happen."

When twenty children and six staff died at the hands of a shooter in Newtown, a well-known radio personality attributed it to God who has "allowed judgment to fall upon us" for accepting things like abortion and gay marriage. Another radio pastor/politician said that God "chose not to stop the slaughter of these young innocents" because "we are keeping God out of schools."

Such extreme statements by self-appointed spokes-persons get widespread press coverage. And after any major disaster you can go on the Internet and read a wide variety of theological justifications, all attempting—like Job's friends?—to explain what happened as an expression of God's plan. ("Consider now," Eliphaz urged Job, "Who, being innocent, has ever perished? Where were the upright ever destroyed?"—unaware at that point that he was participating in a drama of refutation.) Theories ascribing disasters to God's judgment end up sounding more like karma than providence. Why do we continue to think that good and evil, pain and pleasure, are doled out according to our merit when the Book of Job teaches just the opposite?

Committed Calvinists strain to explain catastrophes, along with everything else, as an expression of God's sovereign will. I follow their arguments with some sympathy, yet wonder why Jesus never used such reasoning with the suffering people he encountered. Never do I see Jesus lecturing people on the need to accept blindness or lameness as an expression of God's secret will; rather, he healed them. He taught us to pray, "Your will be done, on earth as it is in heaven," and directed us to work diligently toward that goal. Since we anticipate no wars, gun violence, terrorist acts, or natural disasters in heaven—indeed, no tears or death—I choose to speak of God's *desire* for humans on earth, leaving the intricacies of "God's will" to the theologians. The aftermath of a catastrophe is probably the worst time to quote, "God is on the throne."

Words, no matter how well-intentioned, may heap more pain on an already sad situation. "There must be a reason," we say when a family loses a job and sees their house go into foreclosure—yes, but what reason makes sense at such a time? "God doesn't put on us more than we can bear" sounds hollow to someone at the breaking point. Kevin Costner's movie *The War* includes a scene with another spiritual cliché. After a Vietnam veteran dies in a mining accident trying to save a friend's life, his wife tries to comfort their son. "God needed him home," she says. The son yells to sky: "Yeah, but I need him more than you do!" I prefer (and think more theologically correct) the reaction of the pastor at the funeral in Chicago, "Damn you, death!" If we are upset about the condition of this planet, I can only imagine how God feels.

Even a spiritual truth like "All things work together for good" can hit like a hammer blow if presented at the wrong time. Those who speak of suffering producing a greater good offer scant solace to ordinary people grieving their losses and wondering how to resume life. An angry woman recently wrote me about the "hijacking" of her mother's funeral: "There were the missionaries who came up to me right after the service to tell me with a smile that 'if one person accepted Christ during the service, then your mother's death was worth it.'"

After the fertilizer plant explosion in Texas, CNN interviewed a woman who survived the collapse of her nursing home. "I thank my guardian angels," she said, an understandable sentiment. I could not help wondering, though, how that comment sounded to the families of those who had not survived. Then I came across the story of Joe Berti, who crossed the finish line of the Boston Marathon just seconds before the first bomb went off. After several frantic hours trying to reunite with his family in the confusion, he flew home to Texas, where two days later on a business trip he witnessed the explosion of the fertilizer factory, a blast that rocked his car and rained debris around him. Some called him the unluckiest man alive; some called him the luckiest.

Berti's wife had a wise and balanced reaction. "We're grateful that God has been merciful to us," she said. "We are just praying for the people who were so much less fortunate than we were."

After spending time in Japan and Newtown, I have adopted a two-part test I keep in mind before offering counsel to a suffering person. First, I ask myself how these words would sound to a mother who kissed her daughter goodbye as she put her on the school bus and then later that day was called to identify her bloody body. Would my words bring comfort or compound the pain? Then I ask myself what Jesus would say to that mother. Few theological explanations pass those tests. The only way I know to respond with comfort and healing, as Jesus did, is to fully embrace the mother's grief and to assure her that God feels more grieved than she does. In the words of David Bentley Hart, who *is* a theologian, "When I see the death of a child, I do not see the face of God but the face of his enemy ... and that rather than showing us how the tears of a small girl suffering in the dark were necessary for the building of the Kingdom, he will instead raise her up and wipe away all tears from her eyes."

In sum, I avoid trying to answer the *Why?* question because any attempt will inevitably fall short and may even rub salt in an open wound. As Jesus' followers, we can instead offer a loving and sympathetic presence that may help bind wounds and heal a broken heart. Thankfully, I have seen the church do just that. I went to Newtown at the invitation of a church that sent four counselors to the firehouse where anxious parents awaited news of their children's fate and that has raised a large sum of money to provide ongoing counseling for the families. Since the tragedy, six mothers of slain children have begun participating in regular gatherings at that church, one of many that reached out to them.

In Japan I met teams from the Philippines, Germany, Singapore, and the U.S. involved in reconstruction. Organizations such as Habitat for Humanity and Samaritan's Purse mobilized immediately after the earthquake and a year later were still sending crews to aid in recovery. Although the church in Japan represents only one percent of the population, Christian organizations took a lead in rebuilding efforts, and some Japanese churches became distribution centers for food and supplies. One church sheltered more than a thousand evacuees the first few months after the tsunami.

I met some of the retired contractors and construction workers who had signed on with Samaritan's Purse to rebuild houses swept away by the tsunami. They were living in cramped communal housing and working long hours without pay. "We don't proselytize," one told me. "We don't need to — the people know why we're here. We're simply followers of Jesus trying to live out his commands. Just before handing owners the key to their new home, we ask if we can pray a blessing on the house. So far no one has turned us down."

As a counterbalance to the list of seven deadly sins, the church in the Middle Ages came up with a list of seven works of mercy: to feed the hungry, give drink to the thirsty, clothe the naked, house the homeless, visit the sick, ransom the captive, bury the dead. Every day a small army of relief workers and volunteers in Tohoku put into practice those works of mercy. Not all of us can serve on the front lines of mercy, however. As I reminded the staff of my publisher in Tokyo the day I left, the church later came up with an additional list of *spiritual* works of mercy: to instruct the ignorant, counsel the doubtful, admonish sinners, bear wrongs patiently, forgive offences willingly, comfort the afflicted, pray for the living and the dead. The church in Japan, a tiny minority in a distressed nation, is endeavoring to practice those less-visible works as well.

John Marks, a producer for television's *60 Minutes*, went on a two-year quest to investigate evangelicals, the group he had grown up among and later rejected. He wrote a book about the quest called *Reasons to Believe: One Man's Journey Among the Evangelicals and the Faith He Left Behind*. The church's response to Hurricane Katrina turned the corner for him and became a key reason to believe. One Baptist church in Baton Rouge fed 16,000 people a day for weeks; another housed 700 homeless evacuees. Years after the hurricane, and long after federal assistance had dried up, a network of churches in surrounding states was still sending regular teams to help rebuild houses. Most impressively to Marks, all these church efforts crossed racial lines and barriers in the Deep South. As one worker told him, "We had whites, blacks, Hispanics, Vietnamese, good old Cajun.... We just tried to say, 'Hey, let's help people. This is our state. We'll let everybody else sort out that other stuff. We've got to cook some rice.'"

Marks concludes,

I would argue that this was a watershed moment in the history of American Christianity ... nothing spoke more eloquently to believers, and to nonbelievers who were paying attention, than the success of a population of believing volunteers measured against the massive and near-total collapse of secular government efforts. The storm laid bare an unmistakable truth. More and more Christians have decided that the only way to reconquer America is through service. The faith no longer travels by the word. It moves by the deed.

PART 3

When God Overslept

n October 2012 I made an author trip to the Balkans, the troubled region that descended into civil war as Yugoslavia split apart. "Would you like to make a detour to Sarajevo?" asked my Croatian publisher one morning. "That city could really use a talk on 'Where is God when it hurts?'" Recognizing the name *Sarajevo* from the wars of the 1990s, and curious to learn more, I quickly agreed.

As we were driving along the highway from Croatia to Bosnia, traffic came to a sudden stop. Car doors opened, drivers stepped outside for a smoke, and everyone speculated on what might have caused the backup. An accident? Road work? No, as it turned out; personnel were sweeping the adjacent fields for mines left over from the war that ended nearly two decades ago. "Welcome to the former Yugoslavia!" said my wry host. Combatants planted more than five million mines during the war, and they continue to maim or kill unsuspecting farmers, hikers, and children at play.

When we finally reached the Bosnian border, the world outside the car window changed abruptly. A four-lane superhighway narrowed to a windy, potholed two-lane road. Billboards and street signs began to use both the Roman alphabet of Western Europe and the Cyrillic alphabet of the

East. Most surprising to me, half the houses sat vacant, their windows blown out and their interiors gutted by fire. "Yeah, that's a reminder of the Serbs' ethnic cleansing campaign," explained my host. "They forced all non-Serb minorities to leave the area."

"Who owns these houses now?" I asked. "And why aren't they occupied?"

"Probably the original owners still have title—villagers chased away during the war who now live somewhere else. Think about it. Would you want to go back and reclaim a home in the same town where your neighbors raped your daughter and slit your wife's throat?"

The Balkan wars dominated the headlines in the early 1990s. European leaders wrung their hands in despair as the nightly news showed atrocities like those of World War II recapitulated in real time. In a series of uprisings and civil wars more than a hundred thousand people died, millions were uprooted, and tens of thousands of women were assaulted in "rape camps"—crimes that even now are being tried before the International Criminal Court. In Srebrenica, Serbs rounded up every male over the age of fifteen—eight thousand in all—tied their hands behind their backs, and shot them. Workers are still excavating the mass graves in an attempt to identify the bodies.

Eyewitness reports from the court in The Hague read like a litany of horrors: pregnant women cut open, their unborn babies smashed with rifle butts; gang rapes of girls as young as nine; toddlers decapitated, their heads placed in their mothers' laps. "There is only one explanation for what happened," one Bosniak told me: "God overslept."

Who can make sense of the former Yugoslavia? I could never keep the adversaries straight during the war, much less pronounce them, and the villains seemed to change weekly. In brief, communist Yugoslavia had forced three disparate groups together. Croat Catholics identified with Western Europe, Orthodox Serbs allied with Russia to the east, and Bosniak Muslims looked south to other Muslim nations for support. After the collapse of communism the country began to break apart, with minorities rebelling against the powerful Serbs and their expansive vision of "Greater Serbia."*

From 1991 to 1995 Serb soldiers, who inherited most of the Yugoslavian army, took up positions around Sarajevo. The city sits on a strip of land surrounded by forested hills, ideal terrain for a military siege, and the Serbs strangled the city for four barbarous years, the longest siege of modern times. An average of 329 rocket-propelled grenades, shells, and mortars rained down on the city every day, and on busy days ten times that number. Snipers picked off targets as effortlessly as shooting ducks on a pond: a seven-year-old Muslim girl, a seventy-year-old grandmother, a medical worker administering aid. At least 11,000 civilians died during the siege, including 1,600 children. When cemeteries

---

*Croats were among the first to resist. The Croats had no army of their own, just a few tanks left over from World War II and a handful of planes used for crop-dusting. Improvising, they learned to drop propane tanks and water heaters out of the crop dusters onto Serbian forces. To get around an international arms embargo, they released Mafia-type gangsters from prison, gave them trucks full of money, and turned them loose to find a black market in weapons. As a reward, some of these criminals went on to hold high government posts.

filled up, gravediggers requisitioned a soccer field at the site of the 1984 Winter Olympics.

This was modern Europe, where such atrocities were not supposed to happen again. But they did happen, during 1,443 days of relentless bombardment of a city that had no electricity, heat, gas, or telephone service. The main source of water was a brewery that generously opened its deep-spring supplies to those brave enough to dare the snipers firing down on them at will.

Even today most buildings in Sarajevo bear scars from bullets and shrapnel. Plaques mark the places where mortar rounds fell among civilians: 22 died on this corner, 40 in that pedestrian mall, 70 in a nearby food market. I stayed in a Franciscan monastery, now restored, that had received 42 direct hits.

Though Serbs committed the most atrocities, all sides shared in the guilt and had their leaders arrested and tried for war crimes. The wars finally ended in 1999, in part because of NATO bombing and Bill Clinton's peace accords, and the former nation of Yugoslavia emerged as seven separate countries, with Serbia controlling the largest share of territory.

"Why Such Brutality?"

East and West meet on the same street in Sarajevo. Standing in the bazaar, if you look one direction, you'd swear you were in Vienna with its neat buildings, onion-domed churches, and sidewalk cafes; look the other direction, and you'd think you were in Istanbul with its tea shops and a spice market where covered Muslim women browse. Indeed, historic battles waged nearby halted an Islamic campaign to take over all of Europe during the Middle Ages, and no one on either side has forgotten.

The visual reminders of suffering in Sarajevo resemble what I saw in Japan: ruined buildings, wrecked cars, cemeteries crowded with grave markers. Here, though, human beings are the culprits. History staggers under the weight of suffering brought about by human hatred and ambition. This final war of the millennium epitomized an era of conflict and genocide even as it foreshadowed a renewed "clash of civilizations" between Islam and the Christian West. Within a few years the United States, which had intervened on behalf of endangered Muslims in the Balkans, found itself the victim of an attack by Islamic extremists on 9/11.

I remembered a conversation with Bob Seiple, then president of World Vision, just after his return from Rwanda at the time of the massacres there. Standing on a bridge, he had watched thousands of bloated bodies floating on a river beneath him. Hutu tribesmen had hacked to death with machetes almost a million Tutsis—their neighbors, their fellow-parishioners, their school classmates—for reasons no one could begin to explain. "It was a crisis of faith for me," Seiple said. "There are no categories to express such horror. Someone used the word *bestiality*—no, that dishonors the beasts. Animals kill for food, not for pleasure. They kill one or two prey at a time, not a million of their own species for no reason at all. I kept thinking of the verse in First John: 'The one who is in you is greater than the one who is in the world.' Could I believe that promise, looking down on a river scarlet with human blood?"

Mindful of his words, I stood by a river that snakes picturesquely through downtown Sarajevo, aware that not long ago it too flowed scarlet with human blood. I have visited Nazi concentration camps in places like Auschwitz, Dachau, and Bergen-Belsen, monuments to the sort of inhumanity that rattled Seiple. I have interviewed Russians and Chinese who survived the worst cruelties of communism. And now, for a few days in Sarajevo, I met with ordinary civilians in a modern European city who fought off starvation even as their former neighbors used them as target practice in a sadistic turkey shoot.

"Why such brutality?" I asked a journalist who kept a diary during the entire four-year siege. He looked down at his hands, forcing himself to relive those days. Although some of the memories had slipped away, the scars remained. "Why? That's the question without an answer. These were our friends, our neighbors, now shooting at us, blowing up our homes. Philosopher Hannah Arendt writes about the banality of evil. The biggest criminals were good fathers and husbands, people I knew well. They were like the Nazis who would gas Jews in the day and then go home and listen to concerts with their families."

As in the American Civil War, the conflict in Yugoslavia tore apart families. I talked with one man whose two brothers chose different sides. One joined the Bosniak Muslims who stayed in Sarajevo to fight against the siege while the other escaped the city to serve with the Croats. To complicate matters, his sister was married to a Serb who got conscripted by the besiegers. "So many marriages were mixed like that," he said: "Serb/Croat, Croat/Bosniak, Bosniak/

Serb—and so many of them broke apart. Like the country ..." His voice trailed off.

How does a person survive the constant tension of living under siege? Survivors told me you do so by getting up each morning, taking one step at a time, and relying on community for support. Sarajevans lived on a diet of beans, macaroni, and rice, humanitarian aid supplied largely by air from the UN and NATO forces who controlled the airport. It took four months to dig a half-mile tunnel under open fields to the airport, and at night as many as a thousand Sarajevans crowded the tunnel to fetch the rations that kept them alive. The entrance to the tunnel provided a new target for snipers, who took aim at anyone attempting the run during daylight hours.

Nearly everyone, however, also mentioned good times. "I've never had such parties," one survivor told me. "If someone discovered a pinch of paprika or other seasoning, they'd invite all the neighbors over for a party. For nine days in a row my family ate plain pasta. We had no spices, no meat, no flavoring. My mother was so desperate for flavor that she went out and gathered some grass to sprinkle in, just to add a bit of variety and color. Naturally, we shared that dish too with our neighbors." Surveys of elderly Brits who lived in London during the Blitz show that the majority of them look back on those days nostalgically: as German bombers droned overhead, they retreated to tube stations where they sang patriotic songs, cheered the Royal Air Force defenders, and set up cots for sleeping. Something similar happened in Sarajevo.

A joke went around the city: "Do you know the difference between an optimist and a pessimist? A pessimist says,

'Oh dear, things can't possibly get any worse.' An optimist says, 'Don't be so sad. Things can always get worse.'"

A woman I interviewed recalled, "Winters were the worst. Without electricity we had no heat, and we would burn anything at hand to stay warm. I had a newborn baby, born in the midst of that hell. We chopped up heirloom furniture with an axe. You go numb after a while, emotionally as well as physically. Then on Christmas Day a neighbor brought me a priceless gift: the dirt-covered root system of a tree he had found somewhere. I cried. He was Muslim, didn't even celebrate Christmas, yet he sacrificed to keep us warm. I have never received a gift that meant so much, and I still have that hunk of tree. I could not burn it. I tell you with shame, that gesture moved me more than hearing that thirty more people died."

A brave cellist raised the morale of the entire city by his response to a massacre of twenty-two civilians who had been waiting in line for bread. For twenty-two straight days he emerged from his apartment dressed in tuxedo and top hat, set up a stool at the site of the mortar attack, and delivered a solo concert in memory of those who died. His singular courage emboldened a crowd of Sarajevans to join him, even on days when shells were falling close by.

A World Blind and Toothless

As the months ground on, a city that had always taken pride in its diversity splintered apart, like the rest of the country. Before the war Sarajevo had a variety of ethnic groups and large populations of Christians, Muslims, and Orthodox; now the city is 80 percent Muslim, with greatly reduced

Orthodox and Catholic populations and only a sprinkling of Protestants. As part of each conversation I always asked, "What about now—are you ready for reconciliation?" Not one person answered yes. The wounds are at once too fresh and too old, for these disputes go back more than seven centuries. "Every compromise is defeat," said one Serbian leader. And another: "Any reconciliation is betrayal."

Conflict in the Balkans could erupt again. As I write, civil war in Syria dominates the news, a reprise of the type of atrocities I heard about in the Balkans. Genocide played out in Rwanda and continues today in the Democratic Republic of Congo and in Nigeria. I recall Gandhi's remark that if you take the principle "an eye for an eye and a tooth for a tooth" to its logical conclusion, eventually the whole world will go blind and toothless. I have never visited a place in such need of grace and forgiveness, yet so resistant to it. Healing can take place after bitter human conflict—as shown in the United States after our Civil War, and in our close relations with former enemies Germany and Japan—but only if both parties desire it. All too often, pride and revenge get in the way.

One afternoon in Sarajevo I was escorted by a cheerful Franciscan monk named Ivo Markovic. He drove me to the Jewish cemetery on a hill high above the city, one of the main lookout posts for Serb snipers during the siege. Huddled against a cold west wind, we looked down the same sightlines from which they had daily picked their prey. Every plot had been desecrated in some way, the gravestones pockmarked by bullets, defaced with graffiti, broken and overturned. I had read of Markovic in Miroslav Volf's book *Free of Charge*. In his village, Muslim Bosniaks were the villains, massacring 21 men including 9 members of the Markovic family—all senior citizens, his 71-year-old father the youngest of them.

After the war stopped, Father Markovic visited his home village. I will let Volf tell the story:

Occupying the house in which his brother used to live was a fierce Muslim woman. He [Markovic] was warned not to go there because she brandished a rifle to protect her new home. He went anyway. As he approached the house she was waiting for him, cigarette in her mouth and rifle cocked. She barked: "Go away or I'll shoot you." "No, you won't shoot me," said Father Markovic in a gentle but firm voice, "you'll make a cup of coffee for me." She stared at him for a while, then slowly put the rifle down and went to the kitchen. Taking the last bit of coffee she had, she mixed in some already used grounds to make enough coffee for two cups. And they, deadly enemies, began to talk as they partook in the ancient ritual of hospitality: drinking coffee together. She told him of her loneliness, of the home she had lost, of the son who never returned from the battlefield. When Father Markovic returned a month later she told him: "I rejoice at seeing you as much as if my son had returned home."

Did they talk about forgiveness? I don't know. And in a sense, it doesn't matter. He, the victim, came to her asking for her hospitality in his brother's home, which she unrightfully possessed. And she responded. Though she greeted him with a rifle, she gave him a gift and came to rejoice at his presence. The humble, tenuous beginnings of a journey toward embrace were enacted through a ritual of coffee drinking. If the journey continues, it will lead through the difficult terrain of forgiveness.

Not until I returned home from Sarajevo did I realize the significance of the setting of the Jewish cemetery I visited with Father Markovic. "Strangely enough, the Jewish community in Sarajevo once thrived," Markovic told me, gesturing around us at the Jewish stars etched in the cemetery ruins. "When the Spanish Inquisition drove Jews from Spain and Portugal, the Muslim Ottoman empire welcomed them. They prospered here, as you can tell by the quality of the marble gravestones that have since been desecrated."

At one point Jews numbered 20,000, one-fifth the population of Sarajevo, which earned the nickname Little Jerusalem because of its multicultural diversity. By the mid-nineteenth century every doctor in the city was Jewish, and fifteen synagogues flourished. Then, a hundred years later, came the Holocaust, in which 85 percent of Sarajevo's Jews perished.

Cries for Help

From every corner of Sarajevo I heard ghostly echoes of the question that haunts human history: Why doesn't God intervene? Why not take out Hitler before he turned on the Jews? Why not rescue Sarajevo after four days, not four years? "Ah, it is a strange world," said one of the characters in Chaim Potok's *My Name is Asher Lev*. "Sometimes I think the Master of the Universe has another world to take care of, and He neglects this world, God forbid."

I began to see Balkan history as the archetype of minorities being oppressed—the perennial fate of the Jews and a theme that recurs throughout the Bible. Israel too knew civil war. David led a revolt during the reign of its first king, Saul, only to be challenged later by his own son Absalom. Two generations later the nation split in two, ushering in a period of instability not unlike that of the Balkans.

During such times, songs of protest mixed with songs of praise, as seen in the book of Psalms. Eugene Peterson, who translated a paraphrase of the Bible known as *The Message*, estimates that two-thirds of the Psalms are psalms of lament. "I am worn out calling for help; my throat is parched. My eyes fail, looking for my God," complains one psalm, attributed to David. "It is time for you to act, LORD; your law is being broken," pleads another. God seems to understand fully the grounds of our protest as well as our need to rage against the pain.*

At times God's "chosen people," like the residents of Sarajevo, found themselves literally besieged. After one such assault the Assyrians slaughtered thousands of Israelites and hammered iron hooks through the survivors' noses or lower lips to lead them away as slaves—hence "the lost tribes of Israel." Babylon, the next foreign invader, went even further, conquering Jerusalem and destroying the temple of God. When the dust settled, Israelites were scattered across the earth, not to be reunited as an independent nation for twenty-

---

*My pastor in Colorado once took a course on Psalms from Eugene Peterson at Regent College. "I loved the course," he told me, "but I hated the homework. Peterson required us to go outdoors—preferably in the deep forest around the Vancouver campus—and yell aloud five psalms every day, as if hurling them at the heavens."

five centuries. A psalm written in the wake of that tragedy captures the tone of bitterness I heard from Sarajevans about their enemies: "Daughter Babylon, doomed to destruction, happy is the one who repays you according to what you have done to us. Happy is the one who seizes your infants and dashes them against the rocks."

The prophets cried out for God's intervention. "I would speak with you about your justice," Jeremiah demanded in a moment of bravado: "Why does the way of the wicked prosper? Why do all the faithless live at ease?" Habakkuk was less subtle: "How long, LORD, must I call for help, but you do not listen? Or cry out to you, 'Violence!' but you do not save? Why do you make me look at injustice? Why do you tolerate wrongdoing?"

The wealth of lament and protest in the Old Testament makes clear that we cannot count on God to intercede directly in human history, no matter how monstrous the injustice. Many godly people have found themselves, like the Israelites, like the Sarajevans, caught up in war and oppression. I think of the millions of Christians in China and Russia persecuted for their faith, and of those who face violence today in countries like Syria, Iraq, Iran, Pakistan, and Nigeria.

From the Bible's example I also learn that we are right to protest against violence and injustice, and right even to call God to account for allowing such a world to exist. When I bear my own small portion of the world's suffering, I can tell God with impunity exactly how I feel. Richard Rohr notes that whereas Job's pious friends spoke loftily *about* God, Job himself spoke *to* God; fifty-eight times Job addressed God directly.

In a similar vein, a Jewish rabbi points out that Psalm 23,

so often used as a psalm of comfort in hospitals and funeral parlors, combines two very different settings. It begins with the reassuring words, "The LORD is my shepherd, I shall not be in want," painting a scene of green pastures and still waters. In contrast, the second scene is harrowing, including "the presence of my enemies" and "the valley of the shadow of death." Yet the first, idyllic scene speaks of God more distantly, using the third person (words *about* God): "He makes me lie down in green pastures.... He guides me in paths of righteousness...." The tone shifts to the more familiar second person (words *to* God) after the psalmist goes through the valley of the shadow. Enemies are still present, as is evil, but "I will fear no evil, for you are with me...." God has come close.

Those few words, "you are with me," reveal the one thing we can count on in calamitous times. Always, no matter the circumstances, we have the assurance of "Immanuel," which simply means "God with us." The Bible includes some accounts of God's spectacular interventions in history, though these are rare and occur too late to save many of the victims. Far more often, God works through changed people to change history. We cry out for God to do something for us, whereas God prefers to work within and alongside us.

As proof, God showed solidarity with us in the most intimate way possible: God's son, *Immanuel*, joined our species. It was the prophet Isaiah, in fact, who first used that word, in the midst of one of Israel's civil wars. "The virgin will conceive and give birth to a son, and will call him Immanuel," Isaiah said in a prediction that Matthew would later apply to Jesus. In other passages, Isaiah described a child who would be called "Wonderful Counselor, Mighty God, Everlasting

Father, Prince of Peace," and who would someday restore justice to the earth.

Into the Neighborhood

Nicholas Wolterstorff, a distinguished philosopher at Yale, found his faith sorely tested when his twenty-five-year-old son died in an accident while climbing a mountain. In a compact and sorrowful book reflecting on that time, *Lament for a Son*, he concludes that we need one thing even more than we need answers to the question *Why?* We need an affirmation of God's presence in our grief. And Wolterstorff found that presence in the one who took on the name *Immanuel*.

For whatever reason, God has chosen to respond to the human predicament not by waving a magic wand to make evil and suffering disappear but by absorbing it in person. "The Word became flesh and made his dwelling among us," wrote John in the prologue to his Gospel. In the face of suffering, words do not suffice. We need something more: the Word made flesh, actual living proof that God has not abandoned us. As Dietrich Bonhoeffer put it, "Only a suffering God can help."

Eugene Peterson's *The Message* translates the verse in John as "The Word became flesh and blood, and moved into the neighborhood." What kind of neighborhood did Jesus move into? To answer that question requires a brief history lesson. A succession of great empires tramped through the territory of Israel as if wiping their feet on the vaunted promised land. After the Assyrians and Babylonians came the Persians, who were in turn defeated by Alexander the Great.

When Alexander died, a series of successors carved up his territory, the most infamous being Antiochus IV Epiphanes, the Jews' iconic villain until Hitler.

Frustrated by military defeats elsewhere, Antiochus began waging war against the Jewish religion. He transformed the temple of God into a worship center for Zeus and proclaimed himself God incarnate. He forced young boys to undergo reverse circumcision operations and flogged an aged priest to death for refusing to eat pork. In one of his most notorious acts, he sacrificed an unclean pig on the altar in the Most Holy Place, smearing its blood around the temple sanctuary.

Antiochus's actions so incensed the Jews that they rose up in an armed revolt led by the Maccabeans, a triumph commemorated in the Jewish holiday Hanukkah. Their victory was short-lived. Before long, Roman legions marched into Palestine to quash the rebellion and appointed Herod their "King of the Jews." After the Roman conquest, nearly the entire land lay in ruins. Herod was sickly and approaching seventy when he heard rumors of a new king born in Bethlehem, and soon howls of grief from the families of slain infants drowned out the angels' stirring chorus of "Glory to God ... and on earth peace."

This, then, was the neighborhood Jesus moved into: a sinister place with a somber past and a fearful future—not so different from what I encountered in Sarajevo. First-century Israel was a conquered, cowed nation. In one incident the occupiers crucified eight hundred Pharisees on a single day. Faithful Jews clung desperately to faith in *Immanuel*, God with us, the belief that, despite all appearances, God shares our distress.

Jesus' own story is one of suffering voluntarily accepted, for he too became a victim of the Romans. A few decades after Jesus' death, Roman legions set siege to Jerusalem, a prolonged struggle that, like the siege of Sarajevo, lasted four years. Finally, they broke through city walls, killing perhaps a million inhabitants in what one historian calls "the greatest single slaughter in ancient history." Jesus had foreseen the outcome and wept at the prospect: "Jerusalem, Jerusalem, you who kill the prophets and stone those sent to you, how often I have longed to gather your children together, as a hen gathers her chicks under her wings, and you were not willing." Once again God did not overrule, letting history take its course.

From Jesus I learn that God is on the side of the sufferer. God entered the drama of human history as one of its characters, not with a display of omnipotence but in a most intimate and vulnerable way. On a small scale, person-to-person, Jesus encountered the kinds of suffering common to all of us. And how did he respond? Avoiding philosophical theories and theological lessons, he reached out with healing and compassion. He forgave sin, healed the afflicted, cast out evil, and even overcame death. From his brief time on earth, we gain not only a bright and shining clue to the future but also a clear example of how we his followers should respond to those who suffer.

Does it make any difference, this assurance of Immanuel and the example that Jesus modeled for us? Surely it does not answer why evil exists in the first place or why some innocent people (like the victims of the Sarajevo siege) suffer while evil people seem to prosper. Yet it does help us to see God not as a remote being, untouched by what we go through on earth, but rather as One who is willing to experience it in person. No other religion has this model of God identifying so deeply and compassionately with humanity.

We go through suffering not alone, but with God at our side. Two stories suggest that, at least for some, this belief does make a difference. In the first, Henri Nouwen tells of a sojourn in Peru when he was asked to lead a funeral service for a seventeen-year-old boy. Nouwen recalls, "I told myself I had to say something to the boy's mother because, imagine a seventeen-year-old son killed—what agony, what pain. I was a little nervous as you always are when you have to go into a situation that is painful."

Before him stood the mother, two other sons, an aunt and uncle, and a grandparent. He thought of what he might draw from all his education and psychological training for such a moment. "I just want to say how much I really feel with you," he began, struggling to speak.

"*Gracias. Padre, gracias. Muchas gracias*," the family kept saying as Nouwen fumbled for words.

"I just want to say ...," he began again, and again got interrupted: "*Gracias, Padre, muchisimas gracias*." Each time he tried to speak, he faltered and they thanked him. Finally the mother came to him and said, "Father, don't be so depressed! Don't you know that the Lord loves us? Here are my sons, and here is my aunt and uncle. Come have food with us, come to our house. We can stand the pain of Tony's loss because God is with us."

The second story comes from Christian Wiman, a poet who grew up in a religious family in Texas, strayed from faith, taught in universities, traveled the world, and then settled down as editor of *Poetry*, America's oldest magazine of verse. At thirty-nine, newly married, he got a diagnosis of a rare, incurable form of blood cancer that sent him on a harrowing medical quest and also stirred a restless search for renewed faith. His remarkable meditation, *My Bright Abyss*, describes the latter:

> I am a Christian because of that moment on the cross when Jesus, drinking the very dregs of human bitterness, cries out, *My God, my God, why hast thou forsaken me?* (I know, I know: he was quoting the Psalms, and who quotes a poem when being tortured? The words aren't the point. The point is that he felt human destitution to its absolute degree; the point is that God is *with us*, not beyond us, in suffering.) I am a Christian because I understand that moment of Christ's passion to have meaning in my own life, and what it means is that the absolutely solitary and singular nature of extreme human pain is an illusion. I'm not suggesting that ministering angels are going to come down and comfort you as you die. I'm suggesting that Christ's suffering shatters the iron walls around individual human suffering, that Christ's compassion makes extreme human compassion — to the point of death, even — possible. Human love *can* reach right into death, then, but not if it is *merely* human love.

Such a realization eases loneliness, says Wiman. In a modern world that presumes God's absence or lack of concern, "Christ is God crying *I am here*." Because of Jesus, we have the assurance that whatever disturbs us, disturbs God more. Whatever grief we feel, God feels more. And whatever we long for, God longs for more.

A Shaft of Hope

To appreciate fully what the life of Jesus contributes to the questions raised by suffering, I need only look elsewhere. Every philosophy and religion must somehow come to terms with suffering in their own context, and in visits to places like Japan, India, and the Middle East, I have seen other approaches.

Buddhism frankly admits "life is suffering" and advises how to embrace it. By learning to live without desires or fear, it teaches, we can disarm suffering and find inner peace.

Islam counsels submission to whatever happens as the will of Allah. Doctors in Muslim countries tell me that parents rarely protest when their baby dies—grieve, yes, but not protest. And a missionary in Bangladesh recalled locals' reactions to the worst natural disaster of the twentieth century, a massive flood in 1970 that killed half a million people. "People were shocked and dazed, surely," he said. "Yet I found little perplexity, few who were asking 'Why?' They accepted a natural calamity as God's will."

Hinduism goes further, teaching that we deserve the suffering meted out to us, the consequence of sins committed in a previous life. The Vedas spell out the law of karma: "Those whose conduct here has been good will quickly attain a good birth, the birth of a Brahman, the birth of a warrior, or the birth of a merchant. But those whose conduct here has been evil will quickly attain an evil birth, the birth of a dog, the birth of a hog, or the birth of an outcaste."

For their part, secular governments respond to suffering with valiant attempts to eliminate it. Health officials eradicate smallpox and most polio infections, and make strides against malaria—only to face new foes such as AIDS, bird flu, and flesh-eating bacteria. Engineers build levees around New Orleans and sea walls along the coast of Japan, then watch unprecedented natural forces overwhelm them. The Iraq war winds down, and violence in Afghanistan flares up, followed by Tunisia, Libya, Egypt, Syria, Yemen, Mali, Sudan. Shootings occur at Columbine, Virginia Tech, Aurora, Newtown—can we ever stop these tragedies? A terrorist bomb explodes in Iraq, England, Spain, Afghanistan, Boston, Pakistan. Our well-intentioned efforts to solve problems end up resembling the Whac-A-Mole game at summer carnivals.

The Christian faith, building on its Jewish foundation, has a view so nuanced as to seem paradoxical. On one hand it encourages protest, even supplying the very words to use. On the other hand, as I've mentioned, a defiant shaft of hope illuminates the Bible's passages of protest. Followers of Jesus stake their claim on the firm belief that God will one day heal the planet of pain and death. Until that day arrives, the case against God must rely on incomplete evidence. We cannot really reconcile our pain-wracked world with a loving God because what we experience now is not the same as what God intends. Jesus himself prayed that God's will "be done, on earth as it is in heaven," a prayer that will not be fully answered until evil and suffering are finally defeated.

E. Stanley Jones, a well-known Methodist missionary to

India in the last century, made a lifelong study of Eastern philosophy and had many conversations about suffering with his friend Mahatma Gandhi. Jones admired the Indians' calm acceptance of suffering; their beliefs, after all, had a logical explanation for its existence. Jones observed that "Hinduism and Buddhism explain everything, and leave everything as before," whereas the Christian view explains little and changes everything. "God wills to heal all diseases," he concluded, some through surgery and medical treatment, some through healthy practices, some through miracle, as well as others that must await a final cure in the resurrection. In every case, however, God can make good use of suffering itself: "There is no pain, no suffering, no frustration, no disappointment that cannot be cured or taken up and used for higher ends."

Despite what some prosperity-gospel teachers claim, the Bible offers no guarantee that suffering will be removed, only that it will be redeemed—or, to use a more modern word, *recycled*. I take used and flattened aluminum cans to a redemption center in hopes that someone will make something useful out of them. I drop off an outdated computer knowing that a technician will remove the gold and rare earths and "redeem" them. In a parallel way, suffering too can be recycled as a contribution to an enriched life.

I have seen many proofs of suffering's usefulness. For example, the Jewish actor Michael J. Fox wrote that the difficult years of coming to terms with Parkinson's disease had turned out to be "the best ten years of my life—not in spite of my illness, but because of it." His affliction forced him to change from an ambitious, driven personality to someone more reflective and understanding of others. "If you were to rush into this room right now and announce that you had struck a deal … in which the ten years since my diagnosis could be magically taken away, traded in for ten more years as the person I was before—I would, without a moment's hesitation, tell you to take a hike.… I would never want to go back to that life—a sheltered, narrow existence fueled by fear and made livable by insulation, isolation, and self-indulgence."

Pain Redeemed

The Christian view of suffering centers on the word *redemptive*. Though the pain itself may give cause for outraged protest, it may also contribute to life—in other words, it can be redeemed. I resist those who assume that God *sends* the suffering to accomplish good. No, in the Gospels I have yet to find Jesus saying to the afflicted, "The reason you suffer from hemorrhage (or paralysis or leprosy) is that God is working to build your character." Jesus did not lecture such people; he healed them. Nonetheless, nearly every New Testament passage on suffering explores how even a "bad" thing can be redeemed for good.

When they wrote to believers who were unjustly persecuted for their faith Paul, James, and Peter all stressed suffering's redemptive value. For instance, Paul told the Romans, "We also glory in our sufferings, because we know that suffering produces perseverance; perseverance, character; and character, hope."

The apostle Paul likened his hard-won accomplishments to a pile of dung; yet even that can be recycled, as fertilizer. The sufferings of Martin Luther King Jr., of Nelson Mandela, of Solzhenitsyn, were all redeemed in ways they could not have imagined at the time. And the hallmark crime of history, the execution of God's own Son, we remember as *Good Friday*, not Dark or Tragic Friday. Jesus said he could have called on legions of angels to prevent the crucifixion. He did not. The redemptive way goes through pain, not around it.

Several weeks after returning from Sarajevo I picked up two books, one old and one new, written by my friend Jerry Sittser, a professor at Whitworth College, who recounts his personal saga of redemptive suffering. Twenty years ago Jerry was driving his family in a minivan in rural Idaho when a drunken driver going eighty-five miles per hour missed a curve, jumped a lane, and crashed headfirst into Sittser's van. In the next few minutes, in spite of his desperate attempts at resuscitation, Jerry saw his wife, his mother, and his four-year-old daughter die before his eyes. He lost three generations at once, and his three surviving children had significant injuries.

Jerry wrote about that trauma in the earlier book, *A Grace Disguised*, which has helped many others cope with their own sorrow and loss. In it he details the stages of grief and the difficulties of coping with life as a single parent while managing a full-time job. He writes, "I remember sinking into my favorite chair night after night, feeling so exhausted and anguished that I wondered whether I could survive another day, whether I *wanted* to survive another day. I felt punished by simply being alive and thought death would bring welcomed relief."

Jerry faced a hinge moment in his life. The future loomed as a vast and frightening unknown. "The loss brought about by the accident had changed my life, setting me on a course down which I had to journey whether I wanted to or not. I was assigned both a tremendous burden and a terrible challenge. I faced the test of my life. One phase of my life had ended; another, the most difficult, was about to begin."

Twenty years later Jerry wrote a follow-up book, *A Grace Revealed*. He tells of what has happened since that time: the practical help he got from students and other members of the college community, the trials of rearing motherless children, and eventually the new challenges of a second marriage and blended family. Each of the words mentioned by Paul—perseverance, character, hope—play a role in Sittser's story, and the early part of the book focuses on the word *redemption*.

Most English words that begin with the prefix *re-*, Sittser notes, hark back to some original state in the past. We re-hab an old house, re-sume class after winter break, re-organize the office, re-discover the pleasure of skiing. The word *re-deem* adds a new dimension by pointing ahead to the future. A redeemed slave is liberated to a new life; a redeemed sinner enters a new state of grace. Yet, Jerry adds, redemption always involves a cost. To redeem a slave, someone must pay—or, in the case of the U.S. Civil War, an entire nation must pay. To redeem a planet, Someone must die.

I would suggest one more fact about redemption: even in the new state, scars remain. A ransomed slave wears literal scars on his limbs and back from shackles and beatings. A redeemed alcoholic carries scars in his liver. Redeemed suffering includes scars too: the accident and its aftermath will never be erased from Jerry's and his children's memories. Tsunami survivors, the victims of war in Sarajevo, the community of Newtown—they may find ways to endure suffering, even redeem it, but the painful memories will never disappear, nor should they. Even Jesus' resurrected body retained its scars.

In the final chapter of *A Grace Revealed* Jerry admits that he cannot end the book as neatly and tidily as a children's story, with a cheerful report that after a time life went on "happily ever after."

Eventually, we will live happily ever after, but only when the redemptive story ends, which seems a long way off. In the meantime, you and I are somewhere in the middle of the story, as if stuck in the chaos and messiness of a half-finished home improvement project. We might have one chapter left in our story, or we might have fifty. We could experience more of the same for years to come, or we could be on the verge of a change so dramatic that if we knew about it we would faint with fear or wonder, or perhaps both. We could be entering the happiest phase of our lives, or the saddest. We simply don't know and can't know....

In my mind, there is only one good option: *we must choose to stay in the redemptive story.* However unclear it might be to us, we can trust that God is writing the story....

Room to Grow

The late Dallas Willard's book *The Divine Conspiracy* includes these words tucked away in a subordinate clause: "Nothing irredeemable has happened to us or can happen to us on our way to our destiny in God's full world."

For me, that phrase has come to summarize the grand scheme of cosmic history set forth in Romans 8. "Who shall separate us from the love of Christ?" Paul asks rhetorically as he enumerates the trials he faced as a harassed missionary: "Shall trouble or hardship or persecution or famine or nakedness or danger or sword?" No, for "we know that in all things God works for the good of those who love him, who have been called according to his purpose." And "he who did not spare his own Son, but gave him up for us all—how will he not also, along with him, graciously give us all things?"

The entire Bible is a story of redemption: of Adam getting a second chance, along with his murderous son Cain; of blessings for the likes of Abraham and Jacob despite their lapses and lies; of Joseph's and Daniel's triumphs after false imprisonment; of balky Moses and lusty David and whiny Jeremiah; and of the motley assortment of murderers, adulterers, and rotten kings tucked into Matthew's list of Jesus' ancestors; of Jesus himself laying down his life for the sake of others. As novelist Marilynne Robinson puts it, "The great recurring theme of biblical narrative is always rescue, whether of Noah and his family, the people of Israel, or Christ's redeemed. The idea that there is a remnant too precious to be lost, in whom humanity will in some sense survive, has always been a generous hope, and a pious hope."

"Nothing irredeemable can happen to us"—I saw proof even in war-ravaged Sarajevo. I stayed at the monastery that had been damaged by forty-two artillery shells, but that Father Markovic and his fellow monks had lovingly restored. While most Christians fled the city, abandoning it to the Muslims, the Franciscan order stayed behind. They serve meals to the poor, help the homeless, and lead the fragile peace movement. My first evening there I attended a concert and multifaith gathering with Jews (several hundred remain in Sarajevo) and Muslims in honor of St. Francis. It was he, after all, who crossed enemy lines to meet with the Saracens in an attempt to stop the Crusades.

The next evening I spoke at a Pentecostal church. The pastor told me of a dark night of the soul during which he felt profound disappointment in God. In the midst of the siege and bombardment, he got a diagnosis of cancer, and a short time later his wife delivered a child afflicted with cerebral palsy. He too decided to remain in the beleaguered city. His church kept growing because no one knew where else to turn. "When God seems absent, sometimes it's up to us to show his presence," he told me. Often the world only knows the truth of Immanuel, "God with us," because of his followers.

By natural reflex we want to flee suffering. At some point, though, we will encounter a difficulty that has no easy escape, the "unavoidable suffering" such as Viktor Frankl faced in a concentration camp and Sarajevo withstood in a siege. Followers of Jesus get no exemption from the tragedies of evil and death, just as Jesus himself did not. Instead, trials can become occasions for the work of grace, by wakening dormant reserves of courage and love and compassion that we may not have been aware of.

John Ortberg once helped conduct a survey on spiritual formation that asked thousands of people when they grew most spiritually and what contributed to that growth. The number one contributor surprised him. It was not pastoral teaching, or small group fellowship, or worship services, or books of theology—rather, they mentioned suffering. "People said they grew more during seasons of loss, pain, and crisis than they did at any other time." We discover the hidden value of suffering only by suffering—not as part of God's original or ultimate plan for us, but as a redemptive transformation that takes place in the midst of trial.

Paula D'Arcy, an author who lost her husband and twenty-one-month-old daughter in an auto accident involving a drunk driver, has led grief groups after major catastrophes such as Hurricane Katrina. "I realized that there are two levels of life," she says in reflecting on her own grief. "One is the small story of your life and the other is this movement of the spirit of God trying to help our souls awaken to a power greater than anything that will ever happen to us. Grief was the opening through which I found that power. In many ways it was a great gift to be broken open at so young an age because it gave me the rest of my life to benefit from what I'd learned. . . . No matter what else might happen, I'd found a place inside that is greater than the darkness."

Growth through suffering is not automatic, of course. Without community support and wise love, suffering can lead to isolation and despair. Yet, as a journalist, I have seen its alchemy at work in many places: among leprosy patients in India, imprisoned pastors in China and Myanmar, impoverished senior citizens in Chicago, hospice patients in Colorado, friends and acquaintances who battle cancer and other life-threatening conditions.

A Scottish woman named Margaret, stricken with throat cancer, had a succession of well-meaning visitors who came into her hospital room with sympathetic comments. Finding it difficult to speak, she wrote these words on a piece of scrap paper: "This is not the worst thing to ever happen! Cancer is so limited. It cannot cripple love, shatter hope, corrode faith, eat away peace, destroy confidence, kill friendship, shut out memories, silence courage, quench the Spirit or lessen the power of Jesus."

A personal friend of mine with stage 4 cancer went even further, drawing a parallel between her trial and the chemotherapy treatments she was receiving. Chemo treatments are designed to kill the bad cancer cells, she knew, so she asked God to similarly use her "toxic, painful trial to destroy, starve and kill anything in my soul that is selfish, unholy, offensive to Him. I willingly surrender to His infusion, knowing that He has chosen what will ultimately bring me more abundant life than I could have imagined." As I read those words, knowing the toll that chemo treatments had taken, I marveled at her spirit.

Yet another cancer patient, a friend from New Zealand, wrote in the midst of chemotherapy treatments:

With gratefulness once again for your prayers and company on this journey. May God's love spill out into your lives in unexpected ways in the next weeks. Once again, that could be merely a pious conclusion, couldn't it? But this is the astonishing thing we have come to know: that the God of the 14 billion years since the beginning of the universe; the God of human history and its long prehistory; the God of the 7 billion rejoicing, suffering, hoping, aching people on our planet, nonetheless meets us personally, listens to what we say, is interested in who we are and is passionate about what we might become, and walks alongside us in the chances and challenges of life. It's outrageous, and improbable, and true.

"Affliction is the best book in my library," said Martin Luther. I doubt I could make such a confident statement. From many witnesses, though, I've concluded that pain redeemed impresses me more than pain removed. We're concerned with how things turn out; God seems more concerned with how *we* turn out.

PART 4

Healing Evil

Adam Lanza was a lonely twenty-year-old who lived with his mother in Newtown, Connecticut, having cut off all contact with his father and brother a year after his parents' divorce. Early on, Adam had shown signs of Asperger syndrome, a form of autism, and after first grade at Sandy Hook Elementary, he was shuffled around from public to private schools, interspersed with stints of homeschooling. Nevertheless, he performed well academically in high school and also in college, which he entered at the age of sixteen, earning A's and B's before dropping out after a year.

On the morning of December 14, 2012, Lanza retrieved two pistols and a semiautomatic rifle from his mother's gun collection in an unlocked closet, clipped in ammunition, and walked into her bedroom where he proceeded to fire four bullets into her as she lay in bed. Then he drove to his old elementary school, shot his way through the locked door, and began a rampage that would shock the world.

The principal and a school psychologist, who rushed from a conference room when they heard shattering glass and a commotion in the hallway, were his first victims. An alert school secretary left the intercom system on, and so teachers throughout the school heard the popping sounds of gunfire as well as screams, prompting them to call out "Lockdown!" and barricade their students behind bolted doors. Lanza passed one first-grade classroom and entered that of Lauren Rousseau, a substitute for a teacher on maternity leave. He shot Rousseau and her fourteen students as well as a special education teacher who had been employed for just over a week.

In that classroom the police would find fourteen small bodies huddled together, each shot at least twice. Officers found one little boy still alive. He would die in an ambulance on the way to the hospital. Incredibly, one six-year-old girl had survived by playing dead. She walked out of the school covered in her classmates' blood. "Mommy, I'm okay, but all my friends are dead," she said when she finally rejoined her mother.

In the next classroom, teacher Victoria Soto had hidden her twenty children in a closet and cupboard. She tried to divert the shooter by telling him all her children were in the auditorium at the other end of the school. Then the closet door opened and some of the frightened children made a run for it. Lanza killed six of them, and while he paused to load another ammunition clip, six more escaped, fleeing to the front yard of a retired psychologist across the street. Soto's body was found on top of the children she tried to protect, along with the body of another teacher who specialized in autism. Students' drawings hung on the bulletin board with captions like "I love my teacher Miss Soto."

Other teachers had called 9-1-1 as soon as they sensed trouble, and police arrived within ten minutes of the first shot. Law enforcement had been well trained, learning from past mistakes such as when police surrounded Columbine High School and waited too long as more students died. This time the police burst in immediately, guns drawn, in a wedge formation. By now Lanza had gone through several thirty-round clips from his Bushmaster rifle. As police charged in with sirens blaring outside, the shooter turned a handgun on himself.

A few minutes later the police searched a cabinet in Soto's room and were startled to find seven sets of eyes staring back at them—the children who had stayed in the dark cupboard while mayhem went on around them. Down the hall, a terrified teacher refused to unlock her classroom door until an officer shoved his badge under it. She opened the door to find fifteen state cops and federal agents with automatic rifles.

Twelve girls and eight boys, all aged six or seven, lay dead, as well as six educators. After conducting a sweep of the school, police escorted the four hundred surviving children, directing them to place their hands on the shoulders of the child in front of them and close their eyes as they walked in a line outside.

Meanwhile, a telephone message had alerted parents of Sandy Hook students to report to the firehouse just down the road from the school. Hundreds of frantic parents descended on the scene, reuniting with their surviving children with cries and hugs. As these families left for home, overcome with relief, the anxious parents of twenty children who did not emerge from the school retreated to the community center for the longest wait of their lives.

Town of Sorrow

News editors had already selected the top news story of 2012, with President Barack Obama's reelection polling the most votes. But after the December tragedy at Sandy Hook all other news seemed somehow insignificant. For the first time ever the Associated Press re-voted, now naming the saddest event of the year as the most important.

Numbed by other shootings — Columbine, Virginia Tech, Gabby Giffords, the Aurora theater — some Americans thought we were beyond shock. The killings at Sandy Hook pierced the soul of a nation in a new, more horrible way. Each night we heard more details about the kids with freckled faces and goofy grins and limpid eyes who stared back at us from magazine photos and television screens even as we watched their small coffins being lowered into graves. *What's wrong with us?* the pundits asked. What kind of society are we, to spawn such acts of violence?

A few days later, while I was still reeling from the news, the phone rang. "Philip, it's Clive Calver," said a familiar British-accented voice. "I haven't seen you for a while, but you remember we worked together at some events back in the U.K."

"Of course I remember, Clive. Then you went on to head up World Relief, didn't you?"

"That's right, the relief agency for the National Association of Evangelicals. I spent some good years working out of your old stomping grounds near Chicago. You may not have heard, but after that I became pastor of a church called Walnut Hill Community Church. It's one mile from the town limits of Newtown, Connecticut, where I live."

The mood suddenly altered. "That's why I'm calling," he went on. "I know you were involved in the aftermath of Columbine, and you spoke at Virginia Tech after the shootings there. Philip, we're the largest church in the area, and we're deeply involved in the tragedy here. We have parents who lost their children. We've had one funeral already and another scheduled tomorrow. One of the first responders on the scene attends our church, as well as some teachers. They're all hurting, and we want to do something for the community. I know it's Christmas time and I'm sure you have plans, but is there any way you could come and speak on the question you wrote about years ago, 'Where is God when it hurts?'"

I knew I had to agree, despite having no idea what I might say to such a distraught community. Like everyone, I was feeling helpless in the wake of the shootings. Now I had a chance to contribute something — though I didn't know what. I quickly contacted my publishers, who without hesitation agreed to donate several thousand copies of my books *Where Is God When It Hurts?* and *What Good Is God?* for the community. A day later, when the church called United Airlines to arrange for tickets, the airline waived all charges; they too wanted to contribute something on behalf of Newtown. Next, I sent an email to a group of close friends, asking prayer for the toughest speaking assignment I have ever faced.

On December 28, exactly two weeks after the shootings, I landed at LaGuardia Airport, met my hosts, and after a two-hour drive got my first glimpse of Newtown.

TV commentators had used words like *idyllic* and *bucolic* to describe the area, and indeed the scene was worthy of a Currier and Ives print. As we got off the congested highway the road wound among Victorian farmhouses surrounded by white picket fences, with blanketed horses frolicking in the pastures. Even the town streets had rural-sounding names: Head of Meadow, Toddy Hill, Mount Pleasant, Deep Brook.

Before 2012 Newtown had two main claims to fame, as the birthplace of the game of Scrabble and the home of decathlete Bruce Jenner. A large flagpole stood on a hill on Main Street in the center of town, and I could easily imagine the scene on the Fourth of July, with families picnicking in the city park as fire trucks and corny floats and school bands paraded by. Sandy Hook, one of the villages within the borough of Newtown, dates back to 1711. This was classic Americana, a model of small-town innocence.

No longer, though. Snow was falling, and the gray skies and leafless trees formed a more appropriate backdrop to what had become the most sorrow-drenched town in America. On some houses, wreaths of mourning had replaced Christmas wreaths. Black bunting hung along a porch here and there, and state troopers patrolled the driveways to protect the grieving families from sightseers and news media. The makeshift shrines of woodcut angels and teddy bears were now covered in slushy snow. Only a few candles sputtered against the wet, and the bouquets of drooping flowers had turned brown. Many shops displayed handmade signs honoring the victims. "Love will get us through," read one. A banner, "Pray for Newtown," flapped from a highway overpass, with the same message posted outside the local liquor store. Words scrawled in large letters on a wall captured the mood: "OUR HEARTS ARE BROKEN."

One grieving parent, a therapist, told the press, "We're not in post-traumatic stress; we're in trauma, right now. We've chosen not to make hard and fast decisions about anything. Some days I want to get up and go outside and get the groceries, and some days I can't brush my teeth. Some days I feel I can be a good parent to my [surviving] son, and some days I just want to stay in bed and sleep." Another said he could not erase a scene from his mind: on that terrible day his seven-year-old son inexplicably got up almost two hours early and ran outside in his pajamas and flip-flops to give his older brother a hug goodbye before he dressed himself and caught the school bus that would take him to his death at Sandy Hook.

During the course of that weekend I heard firsthand accounts of the tragedy from affected families and also counselors, first responders, and staff from Sandy Hook. (To protect their privacy, I will not use their names.) Among the adults I talked to, I sensed no spirit of revenge, rather bewilderment and deep sadness. No one had a clue to the "Why us?" questions, and apparently the shooter left none.

The surviving children were coping in different ways. Anger flared in some: one little girl repeatedly drew pictures of the shooter and stabbed them with her pencil. Others showed signs of panic attacks and anxiety, fearful of going back to school. "Will I be safe?" was the haunting question parents tried to answer for their surviving children, who had cowered in nearby classrooms as they listened to murders broadcast over their school intercom.

Inside the Firehouse

On the morning of the shooting, a call came to Walnut Hill church alerting one of the pastors to news of a shooting at Sandy Hook, where his eight-year-old attended school. He left immediately with another pastor, who sent word back requesting counselors to come and support those who were still awaiting word of their children's fate. The parents had gathered in the firehouse and community center barely a hundred yards from the elementary school, now marked off with yellow tape and swarming with police and investigators.

One of the counselors described the scene. "We came as soon as we got the call. Of course we had been listening to CNN ever since news of the shooting broke. Some of the rumors were unfounded—for instance, they had arrested Adam Lanza's brother by mistake—and there were wildly conflicting accounts of what had happened. Anyway, we knew that many if not all the children still inside the school were dead. A dozen? Eighteen? Twenty? The total number was unclear. But when we got to the firehouse we realized that the parents knew even less. They had been asked not to listen to the news. I was shocked. The entire world knew about the dead children—and not their own parents!"

The *Wall Street Journal* described the mood in the firehouse as "tense and complicated." Various officials arrived, who explained they could not release information until they had positive identification of the victims. Not wanting to subject the parents to the scene inside the school, they asked for exact descriptions of clothing the kids were wearing.

Most of the mothers had dressed their children that morning and the authorities soon got the details they needed.

Working parents had joined the stay-at-home moms and dads in the firehouse. Priests and a rabbi had arrived, along with other local pastors and counselors. Some families were comforting their older children who had been rescued from the school even as they awaited word on their missing first-graders. Cartoons were still playing on a big-screen television someone had left on. The families talked in hushed tones, hugged, prayed together, and waited ... an hour, two hours, three hours. An overweight officer with a machine gun strapped to his chest paced the room, adding to the tension.

Parents, assuming the worst, nevertheless clung to a shred of hope. Finally the governor arrived. He expressed his sorrow, assured families that authorities were doing all they could, and said he would let them know about the children as soon as they had positive ID. "Be prepared that you may be here until the early hours of the morning," he added.

Almost four hours had already passed. While the governor was speaking, someone asked, "Are there any survivors?" The governor stopped for a minute, glanced around, then resumed talking. The person interrupted again, louder, "*Tell us the truth, Are there any survivors?*"

The governor paused, looked at his aides as if for help, then gave the news that no one wanted to hear: "If you haven't been reunited with your loved one by now, that is not going to happen. The information we have at this point is that all the children remaining in the school are fatalities."

The governor's senior advisor recalls, "It was a horrific

scene. Some people collapsed on the floor. Some people screamed." Those outside the firehouse heard the wails and moans coming from inside. One witness likened it to a scene from the Middle East after a bombing when relatives beat their breasts and grief erupts. That was the moment when the parents knew for certain that they would never see their six- and seven-year-old children again.

Faith Challenged and Affirmed

I spoke at two community-wide meetings in the church neighboring Newtown on Friday and Saturday nights. The organizers did not know how many would attend. "New Englanders aren't especially religious, and maybe they want to think about something else," they cautioned me. Yet, despite the holidays and a snowstorm that made roads icy and treacherous, a thousand people turned out for the community meetings and a thousand more for church on Sunday.

To open the community meetings, an ensemble played soft music as various members of the church staff walked across the stage and lit twenty-six candles, one by one, in honor of each victim as his or her name was projected on large screens. Then came time for me to speak. I looked out over the somber faces, aware that they included parents of the children whose names we had just seen, and fellow teachers, as well as first responders who had helped collect the bodies. Newtown was mourning at once the loss of its innocent past and much of its future.

"Let me begin by telling you what I won't talk about," I said. "I won't talk about gun control or mental illness or parenting or the grim details of what happened at Sandy Hook. I imagine you've heard quite enough. I won't be giving much practical advice either—frankly, I'm not very good at that. I was asked to speak on one thing, so I'll limit my remarks to the question, 'Where is God when it hurts?'"

I went on to say that, as I pondered the question after Sandy Hook, to my surprise I felt my faith affirmed, not shattered. I know well the questions about a good and powerful God that rush to the surface when suffering strikes, and much of my writing has circled those questions. Yet, as theologian Miroslav Volf wrote on his blog the day after the Newtown shootings, "Those who observe suffering are tempted to reject God; those who experience it often cannot give up on God, their solace and their agony." The presence of so many in church on a wintry night proved his point.

"You can protest against the evil in the world only if you believe in a good God," Volf also said. "Otherwise the protest doesn't make sense."

Not long before getting the call from Newtown I had read Bishop Desmond Tutu's account of his experience in South Africa. As head of the Truth and Reconciliation Commission he braced himself for a severe test of his theology, in part because "good Christians" had carried out so many of the crimes (apartheid was, after all, the brainchild and official doctrine of the Dutch Reformed Church there). Day after day Tutu heard testimonies from the victims of brutal assaults. Afrikaner agents had beaten suspects senseless and sometimes shot them in cold blood. Blacks had "necklaced" corroborators by hanging gasoline-soaked tires around their necks and lighting them.

Unexpectedly, Bishop Tutu found that two years of listening to such reports helped ground his faith. The hearings convinced him that perpetrators of crimes are morally accountable, that good and evil are both real and important, "for this universe has been constructed in such a way that unless we live in accordance with its moral laws we will pay the price for it." Despite the relentless record of inhumanity, Tutu emerged from the TRC hearings with renewed hope: "For us who are Christians, the death and resurrection of Jesus Christ is proof positive that love is stronger than hate, that life is stronger than death, that light is stronger than darkness, that laughter and joy, and compassion and gentleness and truth, all these are so much stronger than their ghastly counterparts." For me, the events at Sandy Hook served to confirm Tutu's conclusion.

I had also been reading the New Atheists and evolutionary biologists who would categorically reject Tutu's view of reality. Richard Dawkins, for example, who scoffs at religion as "a virus of the mind," says the universe has "precisely the properties we should expect if there is, at bottom, no design, no purpose, no evil and no good, nothing but blind, pitiless indifference." Stephen Jay Gould describes humans as "a momentary cosmic accident that would never arise again if the tree of life could be replanted." According to these and other modern scientists, we are no more than complex organisms programmed by selfish genes to act purely out of self-interest.

"Is that what you've experienced?" I asked those who had gathered in Newtown. Standing before a close-knit, grieving community, the New Atheists' assumptions rang all the more hollow. "I don't think so. I have seen an outpouring of grief, compassion, and generosity—not blind, pitiless indifference. I've seen acts of selflessness, not selfishness: in the school staff who sacrificed their lives to save children, in the sympathetic response of a community and a nation. I've seen demonstrated a deep belief that the people who died *mattered*, that something of inestimable worth was snuffed out on December 14."

In the midst of trauma even a sternly secular culture recognizes the worth of individual human beings, a carryover from the Christian belief that each one reflects God's image. I recalled that after September 11, 2001, the *New York Times* committed to running an obituary to honor each one of the three thousand people who died in the World Trade Center attacks, as if they mattered and were not cosmic accidents in a universe of pitiless indifference. I noted too that after a national tragedy the media turn to priests, rabbis, and pastors while atheists maintain a discreet silence.

Though tragedy rightly calls faith into question, it also affirms faith. It is good news indeed that we are not the unplanned byproducts of an impersonal universe but rather creations of a loving God who wants to live with us forever. In Newtown I asked the familiar question with a slight change, Where is no-God when it hurts? Filmmaker Ingmar Bergman supplies the modern answer: "You were born without purpose, you live without meaning, living is its own meaning. When you die, you are extinguished."

The parents I met who had lost a child at Sandy Hook recoil from such a conclusion. They hold tightly to the hope that the existence of their son or daughter did not end on

December 14, 2012; rather, a personal and loving God will fulfill the promise to perfect a home for us.

Life Cut Short

Still, the issues raised by tragedy do not easily go away. One question echoes through the ages: Is this world, even a world that God will someday restore, worth the pain it encompasses? In Japan I spoke with a woman who, her first day on a new job, left her two children with their grandmother and was now punishing herself because the grandmother was unable to help them escape the tsunami. In Sarajevo I stood on a hill where snipers had deliberately targeted children as they dashed across a clearing to fetch water. In Newtown a young boy asked about his slain classmates, "Who will I play with now?"

Why does a loving God allow such things to happen in the first place? In a *New York Times* op-ed piece about Sandy Hook, Ross Douthat brought up the famous scene in *The Brothers Karamazov* in which Ivan recounts stories of children beaten and tortured and concludes that he cannot possibly accept a God who would for any reason tolerate the suffering of children. Similarly, the doctor in Albert Camus's *The Plague* declares while watching a child die of the bubonic plague, "I refuse to participate in a scheme of things which tolerates this."

Only a suffering God can answer whether this planet is worth the cost. I have a clue to the answer, though, after talking to families who lost a son or daughter. If you ask them, "The six or seven years you had with your child, were they worth the pain you feel now?" you will hear a decisive yes. As the poet Alfred Lord Tennyson wrote after the death of a young friend, "'Tis better to have loved and lost than never to have loved at all." Perhaps God feels the same way about fallen creation?

To the families in Newtown I recommended a little book by the late Episcopal priest John Claypool, one that has consoled many parents who have lost a child. Its very title hints why. In *Tracks of a Fellow Struggler* Claypool writes not as a pastor offering bromides, but rather as a father crying out in agony to a God who seems to offer no solace. For eighteen months he searches for a solution to his eight-year-old daughter's leukemia, seeking out the best doctors, having her anointed by famous healing evangelists, soliciting prayer support from his parishioners and friends. Then she dies.

Emotional relief comes for Claypool only after much struggle, when he lets go of all he will miss out on — his daughter's graduation from college, walking her down a wedding aisle, grandchildren — and comes to accept her life as a gift, one cruelly cut short and yet a gift all the same.

And I am here to testify this is the only way down from the Mountain of Loss. I do not mean to say that such a perspective makes things easy, for it does not. But at least it makes things bearable when I remember that Laura Lue was a gift, pure and simple, something I neither earned nor deserved nor had a right to. And when I remember that the appropriate response to a gift, even when it is taken away, is gratitude, then I am better able to try and thank God that I was ever given her in the first place.

Even though it is very, very hard, I am doing my best to learn this discipline now. Everywhere I turn I am surrounded by reminders of her—things we did together, things she said, things she loved. And in the presence of the reminders, I have two alternatives: dwelling on the fact that she has been taken away, I can dissolve in remorse that all of this is gone forever; or, focusing on the wonder that she was given to us at all, I can learn to be grateful that we shared life, even for an all-too-short ten years.

Claypool ends by asking his congregation, his friends, and his readers for help in reminding him that life is a gift, every last particle of it, and that the way to handle a gift is to be grateful. We treat gifts differently than we do possessions. As a doctor once reminded me, every life is on loan and will return to the Lender.

Just before traveling to Newtown I received an email from a friend in Atlanta who had attended a Winter Solstice service on December 21, the longest night of the year. The church service focused on life's losses, with participants naming those who had died and relationships that had been broken. He sent along the following words from the theologian Dietrich Bonhoeffer, which he said gave him a new way of thinking about the death of those he would always miss. "Nothing can make up for the absence of someone we love, and it would be wrong to try to find a substitute; we must simply hold out and see it through. That sounds very hard at first, but at the same time it is a great consolation. It remains unfilled, preserves the bonds between us. It is nonsense to say that God fills the gap. God does not fill it, but on the contrary, he keeps it empty and so helps us to keep alive our former communion with each other, even at the cost of pain."

Grief is the place where love and pain converge.

Two Universals

In *Lament for a Son* Nicholas Wolterstorff remarks that although we have learned to solve many problems throughout history, "there will abide two things with which we must cope: the evil in our hearts and death." Evil and death pose universal problems impervious to any human solution, and on one awful morning, Newtown, Connecticut, came face-to-face with both.

From years-long conflicts like Sarajevo to minutes-long horrors like Sandy Hook and the Boston Marathon bombings, the reality of human evil keeps intruding on human optimism. My home state of Colorado has seen two notorious crimes in recent years, the mass shootings at Columbine High School and at a movie theater in Aurora. No one could blame poverty or a lack of education for the behavior of these shooters, for they came from privileged families. Adam Lanza, the villain of Sandy Hook, lived in a beautiful home in an expensive neighborhood, and his mother received almost $25,000 per month in alimony. Lanza was an honors student; the Aurora shooter was a top-ranked graduate student in neuroscience. So what went wrong? How can a young person methodically shoot his high school classmates or strangers in a theater—or, beyond imagining, a classroom full of panicky first-graders—at point-blank range?

After every such tragedy the press initiates a blame game. The easy availability of guns, particularly assault-style guns, plays a definite role, and each event spurs new debates and regulations. Yet other gun cultures (for example, Switzerland and Canada) don't experience the same kind of mass shootings. Should we then blame inattention to mental health? The killers at Columbine, Virginia Tech, Aurora, and Newtown gave off disturbing signals that should have raised alarms. Others point the finger at video games and a steady Hollywood diet of violence and torture. Some fault the media and the exposure it brings killers; Adam Lanza kept a spreadsheet detailing similar mass shootings. Others blame judges who banned prayer and God-talk from public schools.

Few, however, name such acts as evil, which they surely are. Charles Chaput is an exception. After Columbine, the archbishop of Denver said, "Violence is now pervasive in American society—in our homes, our schools, on our streets, in our cars as we drive home from work, in the news media, in the rhythms and lyrics of our music, in our novels, films and video games. It is so prevalent that we have become largely unconscious of it."

And in response to the shootings at Sandy Hook, Chaput (now archbishop of Philadelphia) wrote,

> God is good, but we human beings are free, and being free, we help fashion the nature of our world with the choices we make. Every life lost in Connecticut was unique, precious and irreplaceable. But the evil was routine; every human generation is rich with it. Why does God allow war? Why does God allow hunger?... We are

not the inevitable products of history or economics or any other determinist equation. We're free, and therefore responsible for both the beauty and the suffering we help make. Why does God allow wickedness? He allows it because we—or others just like us—choose it. The only effective antidote to the wickedness around us is to live differently from this moment forward.

Our freedom to commit evil is, in essence, Ivan Karamazov's complaint against God. No atheist, Ivan believes in at least the possibility of a good and powerful God. He even grants that God might one day wipe away every tear and resolve the injustices of this world, yet he still objects to such a scheme because of the cost, because God has been too reckless with human freedom. In the novel Ivan brings up a series of heinous deeds—cutting an unborn child from its mother's womb, setting loose a pack of hunting hounds on an eight-year-old serf child, firing a pistol into a baby's face—that its author Dostoevsky had collected from actual contemporary events. Were he writing today, he may well have included the scene of a gunman murdering children in their classrooms.

"Tell me yourself," Ivan challenges his brother Alyosha; "Imagine that you are creating a fabric of human destiny with the object of making men happy in the end, giving them peace and rest at last, but that it was essential and inevitable to torture only one tiny creature ... would you consent to be the architect on those conditions? Tell me, and tell the truth."

Alyosha quietly answers no.

The agnostic Ivan can diagnose evil and the failure of every human system to deal with it, but he can offer no solutions. The devout Alyosha does not attempt a rebuttal, but he has a solution for humanity. "I do not know the answer to the problem of evil," he says, "but I do know love." The novel moves immediately to its centerpiece story, "The Grand Inquisitor," in which Jesus himself is charged—by representatives of the church, no less—with the crime of inflicting too much freedom on people.

Dostoevsky presents the problem of evil in a style consistent with the Bible, offering not philosophical proofs, but rather a story, the actual historical story of *Immanuel*. Choosing not to overwhelm human freedom, God instead joined us in the midst of evil and became one of its victims. Jesus did not eliminate evil; he revealed a God willing, at immense cost, to forgive it and to heal its damage.

Speaking in Newtown three days after Christmas, I read the paraphrase of John's prologue from *The Message*: "The Word became flesh and blood and moved into the neighborhood." What kind of neighborhood did Jesus move into? I asked once again. The Currier and Ives scene of pristine lawns and Victorian frame houses? Oh no—this neighborhood, as Matthew reminds us: "A voice is heard in Ramah, weeping and great mourning, Rachel weeping for her children and refusing to be comforted, because they are no more."

The Christmas story includes a setting much like what I found in Newtown. Scholars speculate that a town the size of Bethlehem likely had around twenty—*twenty!*—children of the age that Herod slaughtered. In the end God too, who "so loved the world that he gave his one and only Son," lost a child. God knows something of the grief that Newtown feels, as well as that of every place name on the map of a planet soaked in evil and death. Newtown is actually a very Old Town.

Tough Questions

Sadly, the fraternity of those who experience tragedy, a club to which no one wants to belong, continues to grow. On my visit to Virginia Tech after the shootings there, one of the disabled survivors of Columbine accompanied me. The students listened raptly to her advice, for she had personal knowledge of what they were feeling and what they might expect next. In the wake of Sandy Hook, the *Denver Post* turned to families directly affected by the shootings at Columbine High School thirteen years before. What counsel might they offer the grieving families in Newtown? Their words, which I shared with the community, apply not just to mass shootings but to all tragedies.

One student said, "The first thing I would say is that there are a lot of people who understand exactly what you are going through. And at the same time, there is no one who understands exactly what you are going through.... What happened to you is unlike anything that has happened to anyone else — including those of us who experienced Columbine."

"I'm not sure what I'd say to you," remarked the father of a girl who died at Columbine. "I found out that sometimes it's better for people to say nothing, because you're so deep in pain that you don't want to hear anything except something that brings your child back to you." He added, "But, if you were to ask me, I would offer this: Over time, the pain becomes less. Over time, although you'll never forget, never get over it, you can move on. And although it seems so distant now, you will feel joy again."

The further advice that survivors gave sounds basic, but nothing comes easily to someone in deep grief. Grieve freely. Cry out when you need help. Accept that some people will say insensitive things. Don't shut out your spouse or family. Take care of yourselves. Breathe in, breathe out.

The most challenging time for me in Newtown came after I spoke, when I sat in an armchair next to one of the pastors and fielded questions from the audience. "What do we say to someone who's lost a loved one?" asked one person. "How can I be a light to a community when I feel so much pain and am devastated myself?" asked another. I did my best with these and other questions, and deferred to the pastor when I didn't know what to say.

"What can we expect in the years ahead?" several asked in different ways. "How can we keep the name *Newtown* from being permanently stained?"

I mentioned the story of Dunblane, Scotland, site of a school shooting in 1996 in which sixteen students and their teacher died. Among the students hiding under a desk was an eight-year-old named Andy Murray, who went on to become one of the world's best tennis players, a Wimbledon champion. As his grandmother told a sports channel, "I think deep within him he wanted to do something, to put Dunblane on the map for the right reasons rather than the wrong reasons." He fulfilled that goal after the 2012 London

Olympics, when he chose to celebrate his gold medal with a private victory parade—not in London with other winners, but in the tiny town of Dunblane.

Later, after returning home from Newtown, I came across this recollection from John Drane, a pastor who lived near Dunblane at the time of the school massacre:

> Once, on the way to the school gate, which had been turned into a place of quiet, I saw a group of youths, between seventeen and twenty years old. I saw them place sixteen candles—one for each child who died— in a circle on the damp street and light them with a cigarette.... They saw me and realised that I was a pastor, and called me with the words, "You know what to say in situations like this." As I stood there with tears streaming down my face, I had no idea what to say. So we just stood there, holding hands. After a moment, I spoke a short prayer. Then the teenagers also started to pray. One said, "I must change!" and, glancing towards a group of policemen, pulled a knife out of his pocket. He kneeled by the candles and said, "I don't think I need this anymore," then hid the knife under some flowers. Another pulled a piece of bicycle chain from his pocket and did the same. After standing together for a moment longer, we went on our way.

Was God in Dunblane? Of course.

Drane's story underscores what Charles Chaput said after Sandy Hook: "The only effective antidote to the wickedness around us is to live differently from this moment forward."

Since the spate of recent tragedies, the entire nation has undergone soul-searching, seeking an answer to what in our culture must change.

One more, final question came from the audience on my last night in Newtown, and it was the one I most did not want to hear: "Will God protect my child?"

I stayed silent for what seemed like minutes. More than anything I wanted to answer with authority, "Yes! Of course God will protect you. Let me read you some promises from the Bible." I knew, though, that behind me on the same platform twenty-six candles were flickering in memory of victims, proof that we have no immunity from the effects of a broken planet. My mind raced back to Japan, where I heard from parents who had lost their children to a tsunami in a middle school, and forward to that very morning when I heard from parents who had lost theirs to a shooter in an elementary school.

At last I said, "No, I'm sorry, I can't promise that." None of us is exempt. We all die, some old, some tragically young. God provides support and solidarity, yes, but not protection—at least not the kind of protection we desperately long for. On this cursed planet, even God suffered the loss of a Son.

Death Be Not Proud

In the movie *Shadowlands*, based on C. S. Lewis's life, his wife, Joy Davidman, enjoys a brief period of remission from her excruciating bout with cancer. The two celebrate with a romantic trip to Greece, an interlude of exquisite grace.

Knowing what lies ahead once the cancer flares up again, Joy says, "The pain I'll feel then is part of the happiness I feel now. That's the deal."

Not long afterward, she dies. And in one of the final scenes C. S. Lewis tries to comfort her young son, now motherless. Lewis clung to a belief in heaven as a drowning man clings to a life-preserver, or perhaps as a starving man dreams of food. He makes a subtle change in Joy's words: "The pain I feel now is part of the happiness I'll feel then. That's the deal."

The apostle Paul, himself no stranger to suffering, staked his faith on the need for God to heal and restore the world, the only solution that might bring justice to a badly tilted planet. Paul's life history included beatings, imprisonment, snakebite, and shipwreck, yet he endured them gladly in hopes of a future state: "For our light and momentary troubles [!] are achieving for us an eternal glory that far outweighs them all." Going further, the apostle bluntly admitted that, apart from resurrection, his preaching and faith were useless. "If only for this life we have hope in Christ, we are of all people most to be pitied," he pronounced with a touch of melancholy.

I read to the community of Newtown a poem by Friedrich Rückert, a German writer who, after losing his two children to scarlet fever, penned 428 poems in a paroxysm of grief. The composer Gustav Mahler set five of them to music in *Kindertotenlieder* ("Songs on the Death of Children"). "Now the sun wants to rise as brightly as if nothing terrible had happened during the night," begins one. How dare the sun break through the dark fog of despair!

The last of Mahler's songs, hauntingly reminiscent of Sandy Hook, ends with the same hope that brought comfort to a grieving mother.

In this weather, in this windy storm,
I would never have sent the children out.
They have been carried off,
I wasn't able to warn them! ...

In this weather, in this storm,
I would never have let the children out,
I was anxious they might die the next day:
now anxiety is pointless.

In this weather, in this windy storm,
I would never have sent the children out.
They have been carried off,
I wasn't able to warn them!

In this weather, in this gale, in this windy storm,
they rest as if in their mother's house:
frightened by no storm,
sheltered by the Hand of God.

I grew up among Christians who placed too much emphasis on the afterlife, as if this life were a kind of pre-death state that we must get through en route to Beulah Land. Thankfully, theologians such as Jürgen Moltmann and N. T. Wright have helped correct that imbalance by underscoring the linkage between our present state and the next. Yet I've also learned, especially in the auto accident that brought me face-to-face with death, that I dare not list in the other direction, dwelling on this life only. I need reminders of God's promise to heal creation permanently of the twin enemies, evil and death. Otherwise, what hope do any of us have?

Job got it right, in the midst of his misery, as he weighed the possibility of extinction: "If the only home I hope for is the grave, if I spread out my bed in the realm of darkness, if I say to corruption, 'You are my father,' and to the worm, 'My mother' or 'My sister,' where then is my hope—who can see any hope for me?"

When I was writing the book *Where Is God When It Hurts?* I noticed a detail at the end of Job that had always escaped me. After Job goes through his time of trial, the author notes, God meticulously restored double all that he had lost: 14,000 sheep to replace 7,000; 6,000 camels to replace 3,000; 1,000 oxen and donkeys to replace 500. There is, however, one exception. Job lost seven sons and three daughters, and in the restoration he got seven sons and three daughters—the same number as before, not double. A human being cannot be replaced like sheep or cattle. Even this ancient story, written prior to revelation about heaven and eternal life, contains clues to a future resurrection. Job would someday receive double as he rejoined his ten original children and introduced them to the ten who succeeded them.

While touring the area in Japan laid waste by the tsunami, I visited a middle school where more than a hundred children perished. Holding up an iPad, my host played a student's YouTube video of the wall of water crashing into the site where we now stood. The high-water mark was clearly visible in second-floor classrooms; many children died on the stairway while clambering toward a higher floor. A year later, Japanese mothers were still visiting that school each day, for every bit of debris washed back on the beaches has been neatly cataloged in boxes that fill the school's gymnasium. Mothers thumb through items box by box, searching for some scrap that reminds them of their children: a lunchbox, an ink pen, a photo, a trophy, a school paper, a stuffed animal.

Whom we love, we keep alive in memory. Every Boston Marathon will pay tribute to those killed and injured in 2013. The World Trade Center memorial displays the name of every person who died. Some Newtown parents will preserve their child's room just as it was left in 2012, and all will keep fragments of memory—photos, videos, favorite toys. We trust that a sovereign God has the ability to do far more: not merely to keep alive in memory but to resurrect, to bring to new life the actual persons of Emilie, Dawn, Daniel, Charlotte, Joseph, Catherine, Jack, Dylan, Lauren, and all the others.

At Christmas time we sing O Little Town of Bethlehem, which includes this phrase: "Yet in thy dark streets shineth the everlasting Light; the hopes and fears of all the years are met in thee tonight." Though evil and death still reign on this soiled and violent planet, the event commemorated around the world shortly after the Sandy Hook shootings represents our best, true hope. Jesus entered this world in desperate, calamitous times in order to show a way to the other side. The last book in the Bible spells out what that will look like: "He will wipe every tear from their eyes. There will be no more death or mourning or crying or pain, for the old order of things has passed away.... I am making everything new!"

After the Resurrection, as the gospel spread across the Roman Empire, early Christians continued to die, of course, like everyone on this fallen planet. Gradually, though, death was tamed, losing its sting. Burying places for the dead moved from pagan mausoleums and graveyards on the outskirts of villages to cemeteries—literally, "sleeping places"—in shady parish churchyards. The move was more than symbolic, for it expressed a profound faith in the promise of bodily resurrection.

John Donne, Dean of St. Paul's Cathedral, buried hundreds during the worst years of bubonic plague in seventeenth-century London. When he thought himself fatally infected, he wrote this defiant declaration:

Death be not proud, though some have called thee
Mighty and dreadfull, for, thou art not so ...
One short sleepe past, wee wake eternally,
And death shall be no more; death, thou shalt die.

The death of death itself is a message that Newtown, and the world, needs to hear once more.

PART 5

Three Extreme Tests

Søren Kierkegaard has a parable about a man who wrote a book on the trustworthy, loving God who sees that all things work together for good. Then some personal misfortune occurs that calls into question all that he believes. Where is this loving God at such a time? Bewildered, the author looks up a preacher who does not know him and pours out his story. As the preacher listens, he realizes he has no satisfactory answers to offer his counseling subject. So he recommends a particular book about the love of God. The man replies, "I myself am the author of this book."

I feel a bit like the author in Kierkegaard's parable as I write this book. Years ago, as a young writer and a fledgling Christian, I explored in print the question, "Where is God when it hurts?" Now people turn to me for answers and ask me to address the big issues that swirl around tragic events. The question, though, never goes away—not for me, not for anybody. We keep groping toward light while living in darkness.

I faced the question again three crucial times in 2012, on three different continents, and in 2013 a string of new tragedies only made the question more urgent. By no means do these reflections "solve" the problem of pain or even begin to address other issues faced by those who suffer. Yet I hold onto my belief that on this one question, "Where is God?" the Bible does shed light.

The first answer centers on the event we celebrate at Christmas, a season stained by the tragedy at Sandy Hook. Because of Jesus, whom the New Testament describes as "the image of the invisible God," I can say with confidence that *God is on the side of the sufferer.* Even in Japan, where few believe in God? Even in Sarajevo, where religion lies at the root of the hostilities? Yes! I need only observe how Jesus responds to Samaritans (viewed as heretics in his day) or to pagan Romans with sick family members.

Years ago I interviewed Dame Cicely Saunders, founder of the modern hospice movement, who more than any single person revived the medieval notion of "a good death." She saw more suffering in a single day than most of us see in a lifetime. I asked Dame Cicely the question of "Where is God?" Her reply: "God does not prevent the hard things that happen in this free and dangerous world, but instead shares them with us all." And because God shared our suffering in the person of Jesus, we his followers have a model for redeeming it, a way to wrest good out of what at first seems irredeemably bad.

To disillusioned disciples who watched Roman soldiers nail the Son to a cross, God the Father must have seemed powerless and uncaring. Even Jesus felt a sharp sense of abandonment. I heard people describe similar feelings of confusion, betrayal, and helplessness both in Sarajevo and in Newtown. Doesn't God care? How can God allow such a thing? Looking back on that day at Calvary, a pattern emerges of God turning apparent defeat into decisive victory. God did not overwhelm human freedom or even prevent evil from happening. Rather, what some meant for evil, God redeemed for good.

My second answer reflects what I observed in the places I visited. Where is God when it hurts? *God is now in the church*, God's delegated presence on earth. The question might even be rephrased, "Where is the church when it hurts?" In Japan I met workers who had traveled halfway around the world to rebuild houses destroyed in the tsunami. In Sarajevo I stayed with Franciscans who remained behind to serve the poor and work for peace long after most other Christians had fled the city. In Newtown the Walnut Hill Church has set up a reserve fund for future needs, such as providing long-term counseling for the surviving children. "We're not going anywhere," pastor Clive Calver told me; "our church is committed for the long haul."

Time will not heal all wounds. Even God will not heal all wounds, at least not in this life. Meanwhile, we in the church have work to do. Some have particular gifts: counseling, medical assistance, building houses, other practical ways of helping. All of us have the power of love. Suffering isolates, batters self-image, ravages hope; a loving presence can prevail over all three. As Maureen Dowd wrote in the *New York Times* after Sandy Hook,

I don't expect comfort to come from afar. I really do believe that God enters the world through us. And even though I still have the "Why?" questions, they are not so much "Why, God?" questions. We are human and mortal. We will suffer and die. But how we are with one another in that suffering and dying makes all the difference as to whether God's presence is felt or not and whether we are comforted or not.... What I do know is that an unconditionally loving presence soothes broken hearts, binds up wounds, and renews us in life.

If the church does its job, people don't torment themselves wondering where God is. They know the answer. God becomes visible through people who live out the mission that Paul expressed so well: "Praise be to the God and Father of our Lord Jesus Christ, the Father of compassion and the God of all comfort, who comforts us in all our troubles, so that we can comfort those in any trouble with the comfort we ourselves receive from God."

The final answer to the question hinges on God's pledge of future restoration. *God is preparing a new home for us.* "I am going there to prepare a place for you," Jesus told the disciples, readying them for their own deep heartache. He provided few details, and I for one am glad. I have never been able to visualize or even imagine what that future state may look like. It too lies beyond comprehension. Rather, Jesus asked for our trust. And if Jesus was misguided about our future abode, then we his deluded followers are among all people most to be pitied, and the words of protest in Job, Psalms, and the Prophets will resound through a vacuous universe for all eternity.

One commentator worried that Newtown had forever "spoiled" Christmas, as Virginia Tech and Columbine had spoiled Easter. Perhaps—but only if you celebrate them merely as holidays rather than as real events, heralds of God's rescue plan for a broken planet. I have an intuition, though, that the parents of Newtown, who will forever experience Christmas as a season of heartbreak, will increasingly set their sights on Easter.

Once more, Holy Week offers the template for suffering. On Good Friday Jesus absorbed the worst of what earth has to offer. Our ancient enemies, evil and death, came together in an act of profound injustice. Yet Easter Sunday gave a sure and certain sign of contradiction, demonstrating that nothing can withstand the healing force of a loving God. The enormity of what had occurred—more, the *reality* of what had occurred—dawned on Jesus' disciples only gradually, in small and intimate gestures: walking along a road, breaking bread, cooking fish. Although at first the resurrection didn't alter much in their daily routine, it introduced a whole new way of looking at the world, validating hope that one day everything will change. Soon that rejuvenated band would hit the streets to proclaim the startling good news—news so good that it had to be true.

Two thousand years later, we live out our days as if on Holy Saturday, the in-between day. We look back on Good Friday and its clear sign that no suffering is irredeemable; we look ahead with unrequited longing for a creation made new. Suspended in the meantime, we get not a remedy for suffering but a use for it, a pattern of meaning. As Terry Waite said, after being released from four years' captivity as a hostage in Lebanon, "I have been determined in captivity, and still am determined, to convert this experience into something that will be useful and good for other people. I think that's the best way to approach suffering. It seems to me that Christianity doesn't in any way lessen suffering. What it does is enable you to take it, to face it, to work through it, and eventually to convert it."

God alone can offer a solution for the problem of suffering that I experienced so starkly in Japan, Sarajevo, and Newtown. The poet George Herbert yearned for the day "when we shall see Thy full-ey'd love! / When thou shalt look us out of pain." Until then we cling to the promise that the God of all comfort has not abandoned us, but continues a slow and steady work to restore what evil and death have spoiled.

Just after the shootings at Sandy Hook, another friend sent me a passage from Dietrich Bonhoeffer. My roommate from college days, who is German, wrote, "I found this in the back of our songbook at the church. I translated it and now send it to you—it makes sense on a day like this." Bonhoeffer, a pastor and theologian, was imprisoned in a concentration camp as punishment for his resistance to the Nazi regime.

I believe that God can and will generate good out of everything, even out of the worst evil. For that, he needs people who allow that everything that happens fits into a pattern for good.

I believe that God will give us in each state of emergency as much power of resistance as we need. But he will not give in advance, so that we do not rely on ourselves but on Him alone. Through such faith all anxiety concerning the future should be overcome.

I believe that even our mistakes and failings are not in vain, and that it is not more difficult for God to cope with these as with our assumed good deeds.

I believe that God is not a timeless fate, but that He waits for and responds to honest prayers and responsible action.

Bonhoeffer wrote this creed shortly before his execution by the Gestapo, which took place twenty-three days before Germany's surrender. Death, said Bonhoeffer, is the supreme festival on the road to freedom. If he's wrong, all is lost. If he's right, it's just begun.

Acknowledgments

This book came out of questions stirred up in three tragic places that I visited in 2012. Soon the first few months of 2013 brought a new series of disasters: the Boston Marathon bombings, a Texas fertilizer plant explosion, an earthquake in China, a building collapse in Bangladesh, deadly tornadoes in Oklahoma. The question of why these things happen—and how God might be involved—never goes away. As if in proof, whenever I wrote about the theme on my website or Facebook, thousands of new readers would tune in.

Above all else, I am grateful to the people in Japan, Sarajevo, and Newtown, Connecticut, who revealed to me their deep pain, in hopes that what they have learned may bring comfort to others along the way.

My friends and colleagues at Creative Trust Media first made this book available in electronic form. I'm especially grateful to Kathryn Helmers and Denise George, who managed the publishing process, and to Melissa Nicholson, Laura Canby, and Joannie Barth, who assisted with the logistics of research and design. John Sloan and Bob Hudson shepherded the book through the Zondervan editions.

These are my reflections on questions as old as history, and as current as today's news websites.

Sources

Part 2: "I Want to Know Why!"

25: *Mac Donald*: Heather Mac Donald, "Send a Message to God: He Has Gone Too Far This Time," *Slate Magazine* (Jan. 10, 2005). slate.com/articles/life/faithbased/2005/01/send_a_message_to_god.html.

25: *Hart*: Hart, *The Doors of the Sea*, 15.

26: *Lewis*: C. S. Lewis, *The Problem of Pain* (New York: Macmillan, 1962), 116.

27: *"If the LORD"*: Judges 6:13.

27: *"Though I cry"*: Job 19:7.

27: *"Awake, Lord"*: Psalm 44:23.

28: *"Utterly meaningless"*: Ecclesiastes 1:2.

28: *"Truly you are"*: Isaiah 45:15.

28: *"Why are you"*: Jeremiah 14:9.

28: *"My God, my God"*: Matthew 27:46.

28: *Lamott*: Anne Lamott, *Help, Thanks, Wow* (New York: Penguin, 2012), 6–7.

28: *Buechner:* Frederick Buechner, *Wishful Thinking* (San Francisco: Harper & Row, 1973), 46.

30: *"the last enemy":* 1 Corinthians 15:26.

30: *"I am making":* Revelation 21:5.

32: *"It is for your good":* John 16:7.

32: *"I will not speak":* John 14:30–31, NIV 1984.

32: *"as in the pains":* Romans 8:22.

32: *"creation itself":* Romans 8:21.

33: *"Who sinned":* John 9:2.

34: *Lewis:* Lewis, *The Problem of Pain*, 116.

34: *Rilke:* Rainer Maria Rilke, *Letters to a Young Poet* (Novato, Calif.: New World Library, 2000), 74.

35: *Frankl:* Victor Frankl, *Man's Search for Meaning* (New York: Touchstone, 1984), 115, 75.

37: *Mead:* Dr. Paul Brand and Philip Yancey, *The Gift of Pain* (Grand Rapids: Zondervan, 1993), 274–75.

38: *retired psychologist:* usnews.nbcnews.com/_news/2013 /01/15/16529522-grandfather-who-comforted-sandy -hook-elementary-kids-says-truthers-are-targeting -him?lite.

40: *touching gestures:* blog.pe.com/schools/2013/01/21/sandy -hook-shooting-update-on-the-handmade-snowflake -drive/

40: *"The presence of":* University of Wisconsin Center for the Study of Pain, quoted in Pete Grieg, *God on Mute*

(Eastbourne, England: David C. Cook/Kingsway, 2007), 275.

41: *Lutheran bishop*: Martin Marty, *A Cry of Absence* (Grand Rapids: Eerdmans, 1997), 180.

41: *"If one part suffers"*: 1 Corinthians 12:26.

41: *"in remembrance of me"*: Luke 22:19.

42: *"Consider now"*: Job 4:7.

43: *"Your will be done"*: Matthew 6:10.

44: *"All things work together"*: Romans 8:28 KJV.

44: *Joe Berti*: bigstory.ap.org/article/marathon-runner -witnesses-double-disasters

45: *Hart*: Hart, *The Doors of the Sea*, 103–4.

47: *Marks*: John Marks, *Reasons to Believe: One Man's Journey Among the Evangelicals and the Faith He Left Behind* (New York: HarperCollins, 2009), 167.

Part 3: When God Overslept

57: *A joke went around*: Steven Galloway, *The Cellist of Sarajevo* (New York: Riverhead, 2008), 70.

59: Miroslav Volf, *Free of Charge: Giving and Forgiving in a Culture Stripped of Grace* (Grand Rapids: Zondervan, 2005), 190–91.

61: *Potok*: Chaim Potok, *My Name is Asher Lev* (New York: Alfred Knopf, 1972), 114.

62: *"I am worn out"*: Psalm 69:3.

62: *"It is time"*: Psalm 119:126.

63: *"Daughter Babylon"*: Psalm 137:8–9.

63: *"I would speak"*: Jeremiah 12:1.

63: *"How Long, Lord"*: Habakkuk 1:2–3.

63: *Rohr*: Richard Rohr, *Job and the Mystery of Suffering* (New York: Crossroad Publishing, 2006), 92.

63: *Jewish rabbi*; Jerome Groopman, M.D., *The Anatomy of Hope* (New York: Random House, 2005), 78–79.

64: *"The virgin will conceive"*: Isaiah 7:14.

64: *"Wonderful Counselor"*: Isaiah 9:6.

65: *Wolterstorff*: Nicholas Wolterstorff, *Lament for a Son* (Grand Rapids: Eerdmans, 1987).

65: *"The Word became flesh"*: John 1:14.

65: *Bonhoeffer*: Dietrich Bonhoeffer, *Letters and Papers from Prison* (Minneapolis: Fortress, 2010), 479.

65: *Peterson's*: Eugene Peterson, *The Message* (NavPress: Colorado Springs, 1993).

66: *"Glory to God"*: Luke 2:14.

67: *"greatest single slaughter"*: J. E. Lendon, "The Roman Siege of Jerusalem," *Military History Quarterly* (Summer 2005). preteristarchive.com/Bibliography/2005_lendon _roman-siege.html

67: *"Jerusalem, Jerusalem"*: Luke 13:34.

68: *Nouwen*: from Sharon Gallagher, *Where Faith Meets*

Culture: A Radix Magazine Anthology (Eugene, Ore.: Cascade Books, 2010), 10–11.

68: *Wiman:* Christian Wiman, *My Bright Abyss* (New York: Farrar, Straus & Giroux, 2013), 155.

71: *"be done, on earth":* Matthew 6:10.

71: *Jones:* E. Stanley Jones, *The Way* (Nashville: Abingdon, 1946), 232–33.

72: *Fox:* Michael J. Fox, *Lucky Man* (New York: Hyperion, 2005), 5.

73: *"we also glory":* Romans 5:3–4.

74: *Sittser:* Jerry Sittser, *A Grace Disguised* (Grand Rapids: Zondervan, 1996), 19–21.

76: *final chapter:* Sittser, *A Grace Revealed,* 260.

76: *Willard:* Dallas Willard, *The Divine Conspiracy* (San Francisco: HarperSanFrancisco, 1996), 336.

77: *"Who shall separate":* Romans 8:35.

77: *"We know that in all things":* Romans 8:28.

77: *"He who did not spare":* Romans 8:32.

77: *Robinson:* Marilynne Robinson, in Alfred Corn, ed., *Incarnation* (London: Viking Penguin, 1990), 310–11.

78: *Ortberg:* John Ortberg, "Don't Waste a Crisis," in *Leadership Journal* (Winter 2011), 37.

79: *D'Arcy:* Paula D'Arcy, "Is There Life After Death?" in *U.S. Catholic* (January 2006), 19.

79: *Scottish woman*: quoted in Greig, *God on Mute*, 159.

81: *Luther*: Martin Luther, "Colorful Sayings of Colorful Luther," *Christian History* No. 34, 27.

Part 4: Healing Evil

85: *Adam Lanza*: CNN.com and numerous articles in the *Danbury News Times* and *Hartford Courant* newspapers were helpful in piecing together this timeline. At the time of writing, the official police report had not yet been released, so this timeline is still tentative.

91: *One grieving parent*: *The New York Times* (January 20, 2013).

95: *"Those who observe"*: facebook.com/miroslav.volf.12 /posts/463923590321596.

95: *"You can protest"*: Miroslav Volf, *Free of Charge: Giving and Forgiving in a Culture Stripped of Grace* (Grand Rapids: Zondervan, 2005), 229.

95: *Tutu*: Desmond Tutu, *No Future Without Forgiveness* (New York: Doubleday, 1999), 86.

96: *Dawkins*: Richard Dawkins, *River Out of Eden: A Darwinian View of Life* (New York: Basic Books, 1996), 133.

96: *Gould*: Stephen Jay Gould, *Full House: The Spread of Excellence from Plato to Darwin* (Cambridge, Mass.: Harvard University Press, 2011), 18.

97: *Bergman*: Ingmar Bergman, *The Magic Lantern: An Autobiography* (New York: Viking Penguin, 1988), 204.

98: *Douthat*: Ross Douthat, "The Loss of the Innocents," *The New York Times Sunday Review* (December 15, 2012), SR12.

98: *Camus*: Albert Camus, *The Plague* (New York: Vintage, 1972), 197.

99: *Tennyson*: Alfred Lord Tennyson, *In Memoriam: A. H. H.* (Boston: Mobile Reference, 2008, Kindle Edition).

99: *Claypool*: John Claypool, *Tracks of a Fellow Struggler* (Dallas: Word, 1974), 82–83.

100: *Bonhoeffer*: Dietrich Bonhoeffer, *The Martyred Christian* (New York: Macmillan, 1983), 183.

101: *Wolterstorff*: Nicholas Wolterstorff, *Lament for a Son* (Grand Rapids: Eerdmans, 1987), 73.

102: *"Violence is now pervasive"*: Charles Chaput quoted in Terry Mattingly, knoxnews.com/news/2012/dec/21/terry-mattingly-why-not-blame-god-for-shootings/ accessed Dec 21, 2012.

102: *"God is good"*: Charles Chaput, "Advent, Suffering and the Promise of Joy," CatholicPhilly.com (December 19, 2012): catholicphilly.com/2012/12/thinktank/weekly-message-from-archbishop-chaput/advent-suffering-and-the-promise-of-joy/

103: *Dostoevsky*: Fyodor Dostoevsky, *The Brothers Karamazov* (Garden City, N.Y.: Nelson Doubleday, N.D.), 226.

104: *"The Word became flesh"*: John 1:14 MSG.

104: *"A voice is heard"*: Matthew 2:18.

105: *Denver Post*: denverpost.com/news/ci_22243944
/connecticut-school-shooting-columbine-survivors
-tell-newtown-families#ixzz2FtHuynqY

106: *Murray*: abcnews.go.com/International/tennis-star
-andy-murray-remembers-dunblane-shooting-massacre
/story?id=17995450#.UYp66bV-p8E

107: *Drane*: John Drane, "Was God in Dunblane?"
Baptist Times (March 21, 1996), 8.

107: *"The only effective antidote"*: Chaput, "Advent, Suffering
and the Promise of Joy." catholicphilly.com/2012/12
/think-tank/weekly-message-from-archbishop-chaput
/advent-suffering-and-the-promise-of-joy/

109: *"For our light"*: 2 Corinthians 4:17.

109: *"If only for this life"*: 1 Corinthians 15:19.

109: *Friedrich Rückert*: en.wikipedia.org/wiki
/Kindertotenlieder

111: *"If the only home"*: Job 17:13–15.

112: *"He will wipe every tear"*: Revelation 21:4–5.

113: *Donne*; John Donne, "Death Be Not Proud," *The
Complete English Poems* (London: Penguin, 1987), 313.

Part 5: Three Extreme Tests

117: *Kierkegaard*: Søren Kierkegaard, "The Author of the
Proofs," Thomas C. Oden, ed., *Parables of Kierkegaard*
(Princeton, N.J.: Princeton University Press, 1978), 35.

118: *"the image of the invisible God"*: Colossians 1:15.

119: *Dowd*: Maureen Dowd, "Why, God," *The New York Times* (Dec. 26, 2012), A25.

120: *"Praise be to the God"*: 2 Corinthians 1:3–4.

120: *"I am going"*: John 14:2.

121: *Waite*: Terry Waite, quoted in *Rediscovering Holiness: Know the Fullness of Life with God*, by J. I. Packer (Ann Arbor, Mich.: Servant, 1992), 270.

122: *Herbert*: George Herbert, "The Glance," C. A. Patrides, ed., *The English Poems of George Herbert* (Totowa, N.J.: Rowman & Littlefield, 1981), 177.

About the Author

Philip Yancey worked as a journalist in Chicago for some twenty years, editing the youth magazine *Campus Life* while also writing for a wide variety of magazines including *Reader's Digest, Saturday Evening Post, National Wildlife*, and *Christianity Today*. In the process he interviewed diverse people enriched by their personal faith, such as President Jimmy Carter, Habitat for Humanity founder Millard Fuller, and Dame Cicely Saunders, founder of the modern hospice movement. In 1992 he and his wife Janet, a social worker and hospice chaplain, moved to the foothills of Colorado. His writing took a more personal, introspective turn even as his activities turned outward. "Writing is such an introspective act that I found myself looking for ways to connect with the planet bodily. My interests include skiing, climbing mountains, mountain-biking, golf, international travel, jogging, nature, theology (in small doses), politics, literature, and classical music."

You can visit the author's website at www.philipyancey .com for more information, essays, events, travel notes, and a blog, or his official Facebook page at *facebook.com /PhilipYancey.*

Also by Philip Yancey

Christians and Politics:
Uneasy Partners (2012)

What Good Is God?:
In Search of a Faith that Matters (2010)

Jesus,
Visual Edition (2010)

Grace,
Visual Edition (2010)

A Skeptic's Guide to Faith:
What It Takes to Make the Leap (2009)

Grace Notes:
Daily Readings with a Fellow Pilgrim (2009)

Keeping Company with God:
A Prayer Journal (2007)

Prayer:
Does It Make Any Difference? (2006)

Finding God in Unexpected Places (2005)

In the Likeness of God:
The Dr. Paul Brand Tribute Edition of Fearfully
and Wonderfully Made *and* In His Image,
cowritten with Dr. Paul Brand (2004)

The Student Bible,
notes cowritten with Tim Stafford (2002)

Soul Survivor:
How My Faith Survived the Church (2001)

Reaching for the Invisible God (2000)

Meet the Bible,
cowritten with Brenda Quinn (2000)

The Bible Jesus Read (1999)

Church: Why Bother? (1998)

The Gift of Pain:
Why We Hurt and What We Can Do About It,
cowritten with Dr. Paul Brand (1997)

What's So Amazing About Grace? (1997)

The Jesus I Never Knew (1995)

I Was Just Wondering (1989)

Disappointment with God:
Three Questions No One Asks Aloud (1988)

In His Image,
cowritten with Dr. Paul Brand (1984)

Fearfully and Wonderfully Made,
cowritten with Dr. Paul Brand (1980)

Where Is God When It Hurts? (1977)

Where Is God When It Hurts?

Philip Yancey

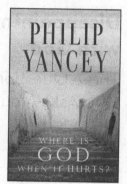

In this Gold Medallion Award–winning book, Philip Yancey reveals a God who is neither capricious nor uncon-cerned. Using examples from the Bible and from his own experiences, Yancey looks at pain — physical, emotional, and spiritual — and helps us understand why we suffer. *Where Is God When It Hurts?* will speak to those for whom life some-times just doesn't make sense. And it will help equip anyone who wants to reach out to someone in pain but just doesn't know what to say.

Available in stores and online!

Disappointment with God

Three Questions No One Asks Aloud

Philip Yancey

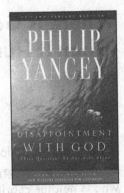

Philip Yancey has a gift for articulating the knotty issues of faith. In *Disappointment with God*, he poses three questions that Christians wonder but seldom ask aloud: Is God unfair? Is he silent? Is he hidden? This insightful and deeply personal book points to the odd disparity between our concept of God and the realities of life. Yancey answers these questions with clarity, richness, and biblical assurance.

Available in stores and online!

The Gift of Pain

Why We Hurt and What We Can Do About It

*Philip Yancey
and Dr. Paul Brand*

In this inspiring story of his fifty-year career as a healer, Dr. Brand probes the mystery of pain and reveals its importance. His work with leprosy patients in India and the United States convinced Dr. Paul Brand that pain truly is one of God's great gifts to us. As an indicator that lets us know something is wrong, pain has a value that becomes clearest in its absence.

The Gift of Pain looks at what pain is and why we need it. Together, the renowned surgeon and award-winning writer Philip Yancey shed fresh light on a gift that none of us want and none of us can do without.

Available in stores and online!

ZONDERVAN
.com

Prayer

Does It Make Any Difference?

Philip Yancey

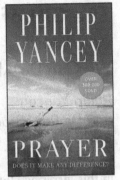

In his most powerful book since *What's So Amazing About Grace?* and *The Jesus I Never Knew*, Philip Yancey explores the intimate place where God and humans meet in prayer.

Polls reveal that 90 percent of people pray. Yet prayer, which should be the most nourishing and uplifting time of the believer's day, can also be frustrating, confusing, and fraught with mystery.

Writing as a fellow pilgrim, Yancey probes such questions as: Is God listening? If God knows everything, what's the point of prayer? Why do answers to prayer seem so inconsistent? Yancey tackles the tough questions and in the process comes up with a fresh new approach to this timeless topic.

Available in stores and online!

ZONDERVAN
.com

What's So Amazing About Grace?

Philip Yancey

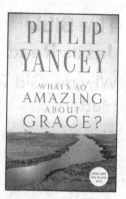

In *What's So Amazing About Grace?* award-winning author Philip Yancey explores grace at street level. If grace is God's love for the undeserving, he asks, then what does it look like in action? And if Christians are its sole dispensers, then how are we doing at lavishing grace on a world that knows far more of cruelty and unforgiveness than it does of mercy?

In his most personal and provocative book ever, Yancey offers compelling, true portraits of grace's life-changing power. He searches for its presence in his own life and in the church. And he challenges us to become living answers to a world that desperately wants to know, *What's So Amazing About Grace?*

Available in stores and online!

The Bible Jesus Read

Why the Old Testament Matters

Philip Yancey

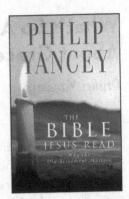

In *The Bible Jesus Read*, he challenges the perception that the New Testament is all that matters and the Old Testament isn't worth taking the time to read and understand. Yancey admits that, like many Christians, he usually avoided the Old Testament. But a surprising discovery awaited Yancey when he began to explore how the Old Testament related to his life today. *The Bible Jesus Read* will give you abundant new insights into the heart of God the Father. And as you read with a fresh eye the prayers, poems, songs, and bedtime stories that Jesus so revered, you will gain a profound new understanding of Christ.

Available in stores and online!

ZONDERVAN
.com

From the Publisher

GREAT BOOKS
ARE EVEN BETTER WHEN THEY'RE SHARED!

Help other readers find this one:

- Post a review at your favorite online bookseller

- Post a picture on a social media account and share why you enjoyed it

- Send a note to a friend who would also love it—or better yet, give them a copy

Thanks for reading!

Printed in the USA
CPSIA information can be obtained
at www.ICGtesting.com
JSHW031023261123
52360JS00014B/282

9 780310 367673